DUE DATE			
			Printed in USA

BOON, THE MIND OF THE RACE, THE WILD ASSES OF THE DEVIL, *and* THE LAST TRUMP

Boon, The Mind of the Race, The Wild Asses of the Devil, and The Last Trump

Being a First Selection from the Literary Remains of George Boon, Appropriate to the Times

Prepared for publication by REGINALD BLISS, with an Ambiguous Introduction by H. G. WELLS

NEW YORK
GEORGE H. DORAN COMPANY

Copyright, 1915, by
Reginald Bliss

INTRODUCTION

WHEN a publisher gets a book by one author he usually wants an introduction written to it by another, and Mr. Doran is probably no exception to the rule. Nobody reads Introductions, they serve no useful purpose, and they give no pleasure, but they appeal to the business mind, I think, because as a rule they cost nothing. At any rate, by the pressure of a certain inseparable intimacy between Mr. Reginald Bliss and myself, this Introduction has been extracted from me. I will confess that I have not read his book through, though I have a kind of first-hand knowledge of its contents, and that it seems to me an indiscreet, ill-advised book.

INTRODUCTION

I have a very strong suspicion that this Introduction idea is designed to entangle me in the responsibility for the book. In America, at any rate, "The Life of George Meek, Bath Chairman," was ascribed to me upon no better evidence. Yet any one who likes may go to Eastbourne and find Meek with chair and all complete. But in view of the complications of the book market and the large simplicities of the public mind, I do hope that the reader —and by that I mean the reviewer—will be able to see the reasonableness and the necessity of distinguishing between me and Mr. Reginald Bliss. I do not wish to escape the penalties of thus participating in, and endorsing, his manifest breaches of good taste, literary decorum, and friendly obligation, but as a writer whose reputation is already too crowded and confused and who is for the ordinary purposes of every day known mainly as a novelist, I should be glad if I could escape the public identification I am now repudiating. Bliss is Bliss and Wells is Wells. And Bliss can write all sorts of things that Wells could not do.

This Introduction has really no more to say than that.

H. G. WELLS.

CONTENTS

		PAGE
INTRODUCTION		5

CHAPTER
- I. THE BACK OF MISS BATHWICK AND GEORGE BOON 11
- II. THE FIRST CHAPTER OF THE MIND OF THE RACE 45
- III. THE GREAT SLUMP, THE REVIVAL OF LETTERS, AND THE GARDEN BY THE SEA . 66
- IV. OF ART, OF LITERATURE, OF MR. HENRY JAMES 86
- V. OF THE ASSEMBLING AND OPENING OF THE WORLD CONFERENCE ON THE MIND OF THE RACE 131
- VI. OF NOT LIKING HALLERY AND THE ROYAL SOCIETY FOR THE DISCOURAGEMENT OF LITERATURE 177
- VII. WILKINS MAKES CERTAIN OBJECTIONS . . 193

CONTENTS

CHAPTER		PAGE
VIII.	The Beginning of "The Wild Asses of the Devil"	229
IX.	The Hunting of the Wild Asses of the Devil	259
X.	The Story of the Last Trump	301

BOON, THE MIND OF
THE RACE, THE WILD
ASSES OF THE DEVIL,
and THE LAST TRUMP

CHAPTER I

THE BACK OF MISS BATH-WICK AND GEORGE BOON

1

IT is quite probable that the reader does not know of the death of George Boon, and that "remains" before his name upon the title-page will be greeted with a certain astonishment. In the ordinary course of things, before the explosion of the war, the death of George Boon would have been an event—oh! a three-quarters of a column or more in the *Times* event, and articles in the monthlies and reminiscences. As it is, he is not so much dead as missing. Something happened at the eleventh hour—I think it was chiefly the Admiralty report of the fight off the Falkland Islands—that blew his obituary notices clean out of the papers. And yet he was one of our most popular writers, and in America I am told he was in the "hundred thousand class." But now we think only of Lord Kitchener's hundred thousands.

It is no good pretending about it. The war has ended all that. Boon died with his age. After the war there will be a new sort of book-trade and a crop of new writers and a fresh tone, and everything will be different. This is an obituary of more than George Boon. . . . I regard the outlook with profound dismay. I try to keep my mind off it by drilling with the Shrewsbury last line of volunteers and training down the excrescences of my physical style. When the war is over will be time enough to consider the prospects of a superannuated man of letters. We National Volunteers are now no mere soldiers on paper; we have fairly washable badges by way of uniform; we have bought ourselves dummy rifles; we have persuaded the War Office to give us a reluctant recognition on the distinct understanding that we have neither officers nor authority. In the event of an invasion, I understand, we are to mobilize and . . . do quite a number of useful things. But until there is an invasion in actual progress, nothing is to be decided more precisely than what this whiff of printer's shrapnel, these four full stops, conveys. . . .

2

I MUST confess I was monstrously disappointed when at last I could get my hands into those barrels in the attic in which Boon had stored his secret writings. There was more perhaps than I had expected; I do not complain of the quantity, but of the disorder, the incompleteness, the want of discipline and forethought.

Boon had talked so often and so convincingly of these secret books he was writing, he had alluded so frequently to this or that great project, he would begin so airily with "In the seventeenth chapter of my 'Wild Asses of the Devil,'" or "I have been recasting the third part of our 'Mind of the Race,'" that it came as an enormous shock to me to find there was no seventeenth chapter; there was not even a completed first chapter to the former work, and as for the latter, there seems nothing really finished or settled at all beyond the fragments

I am now issuing, except a series of sketches of Lord Rosebery, for the most part in a toga and a wreath, engaged in a lettered retirement at his villa at Epsom, and labelled "Patrician Dignity, the Last Phase"—sketches I suppress as of no present interest—and a complete gallery of imaginary portraits (with several duplicates) of the Academic Committee that has done so much for British literature (the Polignac prize, for example, and Sir Henry Newbolt's professorship) in the last four or five years. So incredulous was I that this was all, that I pushed my inquiries from their original field in the attic into other parts of the house, pushed them, indeed, to the very verge of ransacking, and in that I greatly deepened the want of sympathy already separating me from Mrs. Boon. But I was stung by a thwarted sense of duty, and quite resolved that no ill-advised interference should stand between me and the publication of what Boon has always represented to me as the most intimate productions of his mind.

Yet now the first rush of executorial emotion is over I can begin to doubt about Boon's intention in making me his "literary executor." Did he, after all, intend these pencilled scraps, these marginal caricatures, and—what seems to me most objectionable—annotated letters from harmless prominent people for publication? Or was his selection of me his last effort to prolong what was, I think, if one of the slightest, one also of the most sustained interests of his life, and that was a prolonged faint jeering at my expense? Because always —it was never hidden from me—in his most earnest moments Boon jeered at me. I do not know why he jeered at me, it was always rather pointless jeering and far below his usual level, but jeer he did. Even while we talked most earnestly and brewed our most intoxicating draughts of project and conviction, there was always this scarce perceptible blossom and flavour of ridicule floating like a drowning sprig of blue borage in the cup. His was indeed essentially one of those suspended minds that float above the will and action; when at last reality could be evaded no longer it killed him; he never really believed nor felt the urgent need that goads my more accurate nature to believe and do. Always when I think of us together, I feel that I am on my legs and that he sits about. And yet he could tell me things I sought to know, prove what I sought to believe, shape beliefs to a conviction in me that I alone could never attain.

He took life as it came, let his fancy play upon it, selected, elucidated, ignored, threw the result in jest or observation or elaborate mystification at us, and would have no more of it. . . . He would be earnest for a time and then break away. "The Last Trump" is quite typical of the way in which he would turn upon himself. It sets out so straight for magnificence; it breaks off so abominably. You will read it.

Yet he took things more seriously than he seemed to do.

This war, I repeat, killed him. He could

not escape it. It bore him down. He did his best to disregard it. But its worst stresses caught him in the climax of a struggle with a fit of pneumonia brought on by a freak of bathing by moonlight—in an English October, a thing he did to distract his mind from the tension after the Marne—and it destroyed him. The last news they told him was that the Germans had made their "shoot and scuttle" raid upon Whitby and Scarborough. There was much circumstantial description in the morning's paper. They had smashed up a number of houses and killed some hundreds of people, chiefly women and children. Ten little children had been killed or mutilated in a bunch on their way to school, two old ladies at a boarding-house had had their legs smashed, and so on.

"Take this newspaper," he said, and held it out to his nurse. "Take it," he repeated irritably, and shook it at her.

He stared at it as it receded. Then he seemed to be staring at distant things.

"Wild Asses of the Devil," he said at last. "Oh! Wild Asses of the Devil! I thought somehow it was a joke. It wasn't a joke. There they are, and the world is theirs."

And he turned his face to the wall and never spoke again.

3

BUT before I go on it is necessary to explain that the George Boon I speak of is not exactly the same person as the George Boon, the Great Writer, whose fame has reached to every bookshop in the world. The same bodily presence perhaps they had, but that is all. Except when he chose to allude to them, those great works on which that great fame rests, those books and plays of his that have made him a household word in half a dozen continents, those books with their style as perfect and obvious as the gloss upon a new silk hat, with their flat narrative trajectory that nothing could turn aside, their unsubdued and apparently unsubduable healthy note, their unavoidable humour, and their robust pathos, never came between us. We talked perpetually of literature and creative projects, but never of that "output" of his. We talked as men must talk who talk at all, with an untrammelled freedom; now we were sublime and now curious, now we pursued subtleties and now we were utterly trivial, but always it was in an undisciplined, irregular style quite unsuitable for publication. That, indeed, was the whole effect of the George Boon I am now trying to convey, that he was indeed essentially not for publication. And this effect was in no degree diminished by the fact that the photograph of his beautiful castellated house, and of that extraordinarily irrelevant person Mrs. Boon—for I must speak my mind of her—and of her two dogs (Binkie and Chum), whom he detested, were, so to speak, the poulet and salade in the menu of every illustrated magazine.

The fact of it is he was one of those people who will *not* photograph; so much of him was movement, gesture, expression, atmosphere, and colour, and so little of him was form. His was the exact converse of that semi-mineral physical quality that men call handsome, and now that his career has come to its sad truncation I see no reason why I should further conceal the secret of the clear, emphatic, solid impression he made upon all who had not met him. It was, indeed, a very simple secret;—

He never wrote anything for his public with his own hand.

He did this of set intention. He distrusted a certain freakishness of his finger-tips that he thought might have injured him with his multitudinous master. He knew his holograph manuscript would certainly get him into trouble. He employed a lady, the lady who figures in his will, Miss Bathwick, as his amanuensis. In Miss Bathwick was all his security. She was a large, cool, fresh-coloured, permanently young lady, full of serious enthusiasms; she had been faultlessly educated in a girls' high school of a not too modern type, and she regarded Boon with an invincible respect. She wrote down his sentences (spelling without blemish in all the European languages) as they came from his lips, with the aid of a bright, efficient, new-looking typewriter. If he used a rare word or a whimsical construction, she would say, "I beg your pardon, Mr. Boon," and he would at once correct it; and if by any lapse of an always rather too nimble imagination he carried his thoughts into regions outside the tastes and interests of that enormous *ante-bellum* public it was his fortune to please, then, according to the nature of his divagation, she would either cough or sigh or—in certain eventualities—get up and leave the room.

By this ingenious device—if one may be permitted to use the expression for so pleasant and trustworthy an assistant—he did to a large extent free himself from the haunting dread of losing his public by some eccentricity of behaviour, some quirk of thought or fluctuation of "attitude" that has pursued him ever since the great success of "Captain Clayball," a book he wrote to poke fun at the crude imaginings of a particularly stupid schoolboy he liked, had put him into the forefront of our literary world.

4

HE had a peculiar, and, I think, a groundless terror of the public of the United States of America, from which country he derived the larger moiety of his income. In spite of our remonstrances, he subscribed to the New York *Nation* to the very end, and he insisted, in spite of fact, reason, and my earnest entreaties (having regard to the future unification of the English-speaking race), in figuring that continental empire as a vain, garrulous, and prosperous female of uncertain age, and still more uncertain temper, with unfounded pretensions to intellectuality and an ideal of refinement of the most negative description, entirely on the strength of that one sample. One might as well judge England by the *Spectator*. My protests seemed only to intensify his zest in his personification of Columbia as the Aunt Errant of Christendom, as a wild, sentimental, and advanced maiden lady of inconceivable courage and enterprise, whom everything might offend and nothing cow. "I know," he used to say, "something will be said or done and she'll have hysterics; the temptation to smuggle something through Miss Bathwick's back is getting almost too much for me. I *could,* you know. Or some one will come along with something a little harder and purer and emptier and more emphatically handsome than I can hope to do. I shall lose her one of these days. . . . How can I hope to keep for ever that proud and fickle heart?"

And then I remember he suddenly went off at a tangent to sketch out a great novel he was to call "Aunt Columbia." "No," he said, "they would suspect that—'Aunt Dove.' " She was to be a lady of great, unpremeditated wealth, living on a vast estate near a rather crowded and troublesome village. Everything she did and said affected the village enormously. She took the people's children into her employment; they lived on her surplus vegetables. She was to have a particularly troublesome and dishonest household of servants and a spoiled nephew called Teddy. And whenever she felt dull or energetic she drove down into the village and lectured and blamed the villagers—for being overcrowded, for being quarrelsome, for being poor and numerous, for not, in fact, being spinster ladies of enormous good fortune. . . . That was only the beginning of one of those vast schemes of his that have left no trace now in all the collection.

His fear of shocking America was, I think, unfounded; at any rate, he succeeded in the necessary suppressions every time, and until the day of his death it was rare for the American press-cuttings that were removed in basketfuls almost daily with the other debris of his breakfast-table to speak of him in anything but quasi-amorous tones. He died for them the most spiritual as well as the most intellectual of men; "not simply intellectual, but lovable." They spoke of his pensive eyes, though, indeed, when he was not glaring at a camera they were as pensive as champagne, and when the robust pathos bumped against the unavoidable humour as they were swept along the narrow torrent of his story they said with all the pleasure of an apt quotation that indeed in his wonderful heart laughter mingled with tears.

5

I THINK George Boon did on the whole enjoy the remarkable setting of his philosophical detachment very keenly; the monstrous fame of him that rolled about the world, that set out east and came back circumferentially from the west and beat again upon his doors. He laughed irresponsibly, spent the resulting money with an intelligent generosity, and talked of other things. "It is the quality of life," he said, and "The people love to have it so."

I seem to see him still, hurrying but not dismayed, in flight from the camera of an intrusive admirer—an admirer not so much of him as of his popularity—up one of his garden walks towards his agreeable study. I recall his round, enigmatical face, an affair of rosy rotundities, his very bright, active eyes, his queer, wiry, black hair that went out to every point in the heavens, his ankles and neck and wrists all protruding from his garments in their own peculiar way, protruding a little more in the stress of flight. I recall, too, his general effect of careless and, on the whole, commendable dirtiness, accentuated rather than corrected by the vivid tie of soft orange-coloured silk he invariably wore, and how his light paces danced along the turf. (He affected in his private dominions trousers of faint drab corduroy that were always too short, braced up with vehement tightness, and displaying claret-coloured socks above his easy, square-toed shoes.) And I know that even that lumbering camera coming clumsily to its tripod ambush neither disgusted nor vulgarized him. He liked his game; he liked his success and the opulent stateliness it gave to the absurdities of Mrs. Boon and all the circumstances of his profoundly philosophical existence; and he liked it all none the worse because it was indeed nothing of himself at all, because he in his essence was to dull intelligences and commonplace minds a man invisible, a man who left no impression upon the camera-plate or moved by a hair's breadth the scale of a materialist balance.

6

BUT I will confess the state of the remains did surprise and disappoint me.

His story of great literary enterprises, holograph and conducted in the profoundest secrecy, tallied so completely with, for example, certain reservations, withdrawals that took him out of one's company and gave him his evident best companionship, as it were, when he was alone. It was so entirely like him to concoct lengthy books away from his neatly ordered study, from the wise limitations of Miss Bathwick's significant cough and her still more significant back, that we all, I think, believed in these unseen volumes unquestioningly. While those fine romances, those large, bright plays, were being conceived in a publicity about as scandalous as a royal gestation, publicly planned and announced, developed, written, boomed, applauded, there was, we know, this undercurrent of imaginative activity going on, concealed from Miss Bathwick's guardian knowledge, withdrawn from the stately rhythm of her keys. What more natural than to believe he was also writing it down?

Alas! I found nothing but fragments. The work upon which his present fame is founded was methodical, punctual and careful, and it progressed with a sort of inevitable precision from beginning to end, and so on to another beginning. Not only in tone and spirit but in length (that most important consideration) he was absolutely trustworthy; his hundred thousand words of good, healthy, straightforward story came out in five months with a precision almost astronomical. In that sense he took his public very seriously. To have missed his morning's exercises behind Miss Bathwick's back would have seemed to him the most immoral—nay, worse, the most uncivil of proceedings.

"She wouldn't understand it," he would say, and sigh and go.

But these scraps and fragments are of an irregularity diametrically contrasting with this. They seem to have been begun upon impulse at any time, and abandoned with an equal impulsiveness, and they are written upon stationery of a variety and nature that alone would condemn them in the eyes of an alienist. The handwriting is always atrocious and frequently illegible, the spelling is strange, and sometimes indecently bad, the punctuation is sporadic, and many of the fragments would be at once put out of court as modern literature by the fact that they are written in pencil on *both sides of the paper!* Such of the beginnings as achieve a qualified completeness are of impossible lengths; the longest is a piece—allowing for gaps—of fourteen thousand words, and another a fragment shaping at about eleven. These are, of course, quite impossible sizes, neither essay nor short story nor novel, and no editor or publisher would venture to annoy the public with writings of so bizarre a dimension. In addition there are fragments of verse. But I look in vain for anything beyond the first chapter of that tremendous serial, "The Wild Asses of the Devil," that kept on day by day through June and July to the very outbreak of the war, and only a first chapter and a few illustrations and memoranda and fragments for our "Mind of the Race," that went on intermittently for several years. Whole volumes of that great hotchpotch of criticism are lost in the sandbanks of my treacherous memory for ever.

Much of the matter, including a small MS. volume of those brief verses called Limericks (personal always, generally actionable, and frequently lacking in refinement), I set aside at an early date. Much else also I rejected as too disjointed and unfinished, or too eccentric. Two bizarre fragments called respectively "Jane in Heaven" and "An Account of a Play," I may perhaps find occasion to issue at a later date, and there were also several brief imitations of Villiers de l'Isle Adam quite alien to contemporary Anglo-Saxon taste, which also I hold over. Sometimes upon separate sheets, sometimes in the margins of other compositions, and frequently at the end of letters received by him I found a curious abundance of queer little drawings, caricatures of his correspondents, burlesque renderings of occurrences, disrespectful side-notes to grave and pregnant utterances, and the like. If ever the correspondence of George Boon is published, it will have to be done in *fac-simile*. There is a considerable number of impressions of the back of Miss Bathwick's head, with and without the thread of velvet she sometimes wore about her neck, and quite a number of curiously idealized studies of that American reading public he would always so grotesquely and annoyingly insist on calling "Her." And among other things I found a rendering of myself as a short, flattened little object that has a touch of malignity in it I had no reason to expect. Few or none of these quaint comments are drawn with Indian ink upon millboard in a manner suitable for reproduction, and even were they so, I doubt whether the public would care for very many of them. (I give my own portrait—it is singularly unlike me—to show the style of thing he did.)

Of the "Mind of the Race" I may perhaps tell first. I find he had written out and greatly embellished the singularly vivid and detailed and happily quite imaginary account of the murder of that eminent litterateur, Dr. Tomlinson Keyhole, with which the "Mind of the Race" was to have concluded; and there are an extraordinarily offensive interview with Mr. Raymond Blathwayt (which, since it now "dates" so markedly, I have decided to suppress altogether) and an unfinished study of "the Literary Statesmen of the Transition Years from the Nineteenth to the Twentieth Centuries" (including a lengthy comparison of the greatness of Lords Bryce and Morley, a eulogy of Lord Morley and a discussion whether he has wit or humour) that were new to me. And perhaps I may note at this point the twenty sixpenny washing books in which Boon had commenced what I am firmly convinced is a general index of the works of Plato and Aristotle. It is conceivable he did this merely as an aid to his private reading, though the idea of a popular romancer reading anything will come to the general reader with a little shock of surprise.

Boon's idea of Aristotle *(in modern dress) from the washing books.*

(When asked, *"Why* in modern dress?" Boon replied simply that he would be.)

For my own part and having in memory his subtle and elusive talk, I am rather inclined to think that at one time he did go so far as to contemplate a familiar and humorous commentary upon these two pillars of the world's thought. An edition of them edited and copiously illustrated by him would, I feel sure, have been a remarkable addition to any gentleman's library. If he did turn his mind to anything of the sort he speedily abandoned the idea again, and with this mention and the note that he detested Aristotle, those twenty washing books may very well follow the bulk of the drawings and most of the verse back into their original oblivion. . . .

THE BACK OF MISS BATHWICK

Boon's idea of Plato, *from the washing books.*

(Boon absolutely rejected the Indian Bacchus bust as a portrait of *Plato*. When asked why, he remarked merely that it wasn't like him.)

7

BUT now you will begin to understand the nature of the task that lies before me. If I am to do any justice to the cryptic George Boon, if indeed I am to publish anything at all about him, I must set myself to edit and convey these books whose only publication was in fact by word of mouth in his garden arbours, using these few fragments as the merest accessories to that. I have hesitated, I have collected unfavourable advice, but at last I have resolved to make at least one experimental volume of Boon's remains. After all, whatever we have of Aristotle and Socrates and all that we most value of Johnson comes through the testimony of hearers. And though I cannot venture to compare myself with Boswell. . . .

I know the dangers I shall run in this attempt to save my friend from the devastating expurgations of his written ostensible career. I confess I cannot conceal from myself that, for example, I must needs show Boon, by the standards of every day, a little treacherous.

When I thrust an arm into one or other of the scores of densely packed bins of press cuttings that cumber the attics of his castellated mansion and extract a sample clutch, I find almost invariably praise, not judicious or intelligent praise perhaps, but slab and generous praise, paragraphs, advice, photographs, notices, notes, allusions and comparisons, praise of the unparalleled gloss on his style by Doctor Tomlinson Keyhole under the pseudonym of "Simon up to Snuff," praise of the healthiness of the tone by Doctor Tomlinson Keyhole under the pseudonym of "The Silver Fish," inspired announcements of some forthcoming venture made by Doctor Tomlinson Keyhole under the pseudonym of "The True-Born Englishman," and interesting and exalting speculations as to the precise figure of Boon's income over Dr. Tomlinson Keyhole's own signature; I find chatty, if a little incoherent, notices by Braybourne of the most friendly and helpful sort, and interviews of the most flattering description by this well-known litterateur and that. And I reflect that while all this was going on, there was Boon on the other side of Miss Bathwick's rampart mind, not only not taking them and himself seriously, not only not controlling his disrespectful internal commentary on these excellent men, but positively writing it down, regaling himself with the imagined murder of this leader of thought and the forcible abduction to sinister and melancholy surroundings of that!

And yet I find it hard to do even this measure of justice to my friend. He was treacherous, it must be written, and yet he was, one must confess, a singularly attractive man. There was a certain quality in his life—it was pleasant. When I think of doing him justice

I am at once dashed and consoled by the thought of how little he cared how I judged him. And I recall him very vividly as I came upon him on one occasion.

He is seated on a garden roller—an implement which makes a faultless outdoor seat when the handle is adjusted at a suitable angle against a tree, and one has taken the precaution to skid the apparatus with a piece of rockery or other convenient object. His back is against the handle, his legs lie in a boneless curve over the roller, and an inch or so of native buff shows between the corduroy trousers and the claret-coloured socks. He appears to be engaged partly in the degustation of an unappetizing lead pencil, and partly in the contemplation of a half-quire of notepaper. The expression of his rubicund face is distinctly a happy one. At the sound of my approach he looks up. "I've been drawing old Keyhole again!" he says like a schoolboy.

Nevertheless, if critics of standing are to be drawn like this by authors of position, then it seems to me that there is nothing before us but to say Good-bye for ever to the Dignity of Letters.

CHAPTER II

BEING THE FIRST CHAPTER OF "THE MIND OF THE RACE"

1

IT was one of Boon's peculiarities to maintain a legend about every one he knew, and to me it was his humour to ascribe a degree of moral earnestness that I admit only too sadly is altogether above my quality. Having himself invented this great project of a book upon the Mind of the Race which formed always at least the thread of the discourse when I was present, he next went some way towards foisting it upon me. He would talk to me about it in a tone of remonstrance, raise imaginary difficulties to propositions I was supposed to make and superstitions I entertained, speak of it as "this book

Bliss is going to write"; and at the utmost admit no more than collaboration. Possibly I contributed ideas; but I do not remember doing so now very distinctly. Possibly my influence was quasi-moral. The proposition itself fluctuated in his mind to suit this presentation and that, it had more steadfastness in mine. But if I was the anchorage he was the ship. At any rate we planned and discussed a book that Boon pretended that I was writing and that I believed him to be writing, in entire concealment from Miss Bathwick, about the collective mind of the whole human race.

Edwin Dodd was with us, I remember, in one of those early talks, when the thing was still taking form, and he sat on a large inverted flowerpot—we had camped in the greenhouse after lunch—and he was smiling, with his head slightly on one side and a wonderfully foxy expression of being on his guard that he always wore with Boon. Dodd is a leading member of the Rationalist Press Association, a militant agnostic, and a dear, compact man, one of those Middle Victorians who go about with a preoccupied, caulking air, as though, after having been at great cost and pains to banish God from the Universe, they were resolved not to permit Him back on any terms whatever. He has constituted himself a sort of alert customs officer of a materialistic age, saying suspiciously, "Here, now, what's this rapping under the table here?" and examining every proposition to see that the Creator wasn't being smuggled back under some specious new generalization. Boon used to declare that every night Dodd looked under his bed for the Deity, and slept with a large revolver under his pillow for fear of a revelation. . . . From the first Dodd had his suspicions about this collective mind of Boon's. Most unjustifiable they seemed to me then, but he had them.

"You must admit, my dear Dodd——" began Boon.

"I admit nothing," said Dodd smartly.

"You perceive something more extensive

than individual wills and individual processes of reasoning in mankind, a body of thought, a trend of ideas and purposes, a thing made up of the synthesis of all the individual instances, something more than their algebraic sum, losing the old as they fall out, taking up the young, a common Mind expressing the species——"

"Oh—figuratively, perhaps!" said Dodd.

2

FOR my own part I could not see where Dodd's "figuratively" comes in. The mind of the race is as real to me as the mind of Dodd or my own. Because Dodd is completely made up of Dodd's right leg plus Dodd's left leg plus Dodd's right arm plus Dodd's left arm plus Dodd's head and Dodd's trunk, it doesn't follow that Dodd is a mere figurative expression. . . .

Dodd, I remember, protested he had a self-consciousness that held all these constituents together, but there was a time when Dodd was six months old, let us say, and there are times now when Dodd sleeps or is lost in some vivid sensation or action, when that clear sense of self is in abeyance. There is no reason why the collective mind of the world should not presently become at least as self-conscious as Dodd. Boon, indeed, argued that that was happening even now, that our very talk in the greenhouse was to that synthetic over-brain like a child's first intimations of the idea of "me." "It's a *fantastic* notion," said Dodd, shaking his head.

But Boon was fairly launched now upon his topic, and from the first, I will confess, it took hold of me.

"You mustn't push the analogy of Dodd's mind too far," said Boon. "These great Overminds——"

"So there are several!" said Dodd.

"They fuse, they divide. These great Overminds, these race minds, share nothing of the cyclic fate of the individual life; there is no birth for them, no pairing and breeding, no inevitable death. That is the lot of such intermediate experimental creatures as ourselves. The creatures below us, like the creatures above us, are free from beginnings and ends. The Amœba never dies; it divides at times, parts of it die here and there, it has no sex, no begetting. (Existence without a love interest. My God! how it sets a novelist craving!) Neither has the germ plasm. These Over-minds, which for the most part clothe themselves in separate languages and maintain a sort of distinction, stand to us as we stand to the amœbæ or the germ cells we carry; they are the next higher order of being; they emerge above the intense, intensely defined struggle of individuals which is the more obvious substance of lives at the rank of ours; they grow, they divide, they feed upon one another, they coalesce and rejuvenate. So far they are like amœbæ. But they think, they accumulate experiences, they manifest a collective will."

"Nonsense!" said Dodd, shaking his head from side to side.

"But the thing is manifest!"

"I've never met it."

"You met it, my dear Dodd, the moment you were born. Who taught you to talk? Your mother, you say. But whence the language? Who made the language that gives a bias to all your thoughts? And who taught you to think,

Dodd? Whence came your habits of conduct? Your mother, your schoolmaster, were but mouthpieces, the books you read the mere forefront of that great being of Voices! There it is—your antagonist to-day. You are struggling against it with tracts and arguments." . . .

But now Boon was fairly going. Physically, perhaps, we were the children of our ancestors, but mentally we were the offspring of the race mind. It was clear as daylight. How could Dodd dare to argue? We emerged into a brief independence of will, made our personal innovation, became, as it were, new thoughts in that great intelligence, new elements of effort and purpose, and were presently incorporated or forgotten or both in its immortal growth. Would the Race Mind incorporate Dodd or dismiss him? Dodd sat on his flowerpot, shaking his head and saying "Pooh!" to the cinerarias; and I listened, never doubting that Boon felt the truth he told so well. He came near making the Race soul incarnate.

One felt it about us, receptive and responsive to Boon's words. He achieved personification. He spoke of wars that peoples have made, of the roads and cities that grow and the routes that develop, no man planning them. He mentioned styles of architecture and styles of living; the gothic cathedral, I remember, he dwelt upon, a beauty that arose like an exhilaration out of scattered multitudes of men. He instanced the secular abolition of slavery and the establishment of monogamy as a development of Christian teaching, as things untraceable to any individual's purpose. He passed to the mysterious consecutiveness of scientific research, the sudden determination of the European race-mind to know more than chance thoughts could tell it. . . .

"Francis Bacon?" said Dodd.

"Men like Bacon are no more than bright moments, happy thoughts, the discovery of the inevitable word; the race mind it was took it up, the race mind it was carried it on."

"Mysticism!" said Dodd. "Give me the

Rock of Fact!" He shook his head so violently that suddenly his balance was disturbed; clap went his feet, the flowerpot broke beneath him, and our talk was lost in the consequent solicitudes.

Dodd the Agnostic just before the flowerpot broke.

3

NOW that I have been searching my memory, I incline rather more than I did to the opinion that the bare suggestion at any rate of this particular Book did come from me. I probably went to Boon soon after this talk with Dodd and said a fine book might be written about the Mind of Humanity, and in all likelihood I gave some outline—I have forgotten what. I wanted a larger picture of that great Being his imagination had struck out. I remember at any rate Boon taking me into his study, picking out Goldsmith's "Inquiry into the Present State of Polite Learning," turning it over and reading from it. "Something in this line?" he said, and read:

" 'Complaints of our degeneracy in literature as well as in morals I own have been frequently exhibited of late. . . . The dullest critic who strives at a reputation for delicacy, by showing he cannot be pleased. . . .'

"The old, old thing, you see! The weak protest of the living."

He turned over the pages. "He shows a proper feeling, but he's a little thin. . . . He says some good things. But—'The age of Louis XIV, notwithstanding these respectable names, is still vastly superior.' Is it? Guess the respectable names that age of Louis XIV could override!—Voltaire, Rousseau, Diderot, Montesquieu, D'Alembert! And now tell me the respectable names of the age of Louis XIV. And the conclusion of the whole matter—

" 'Thus the man who, under the patronage of the great might have done honour to humanity, when only patronized by the bookseller becomes a thing a little superior to the fellow who works at the press.'

" 'The patronage of the great'! 'Fellow who works at the press'! Goldsmith was a damnably genteel person at times in spite of the 'Vicar'! It's printed with the long 's,' you see. It all helps to remind one that times have changed." . . .

I followed his careless footsteps into the garden; he went gesticulating before me, repeating, " 'An Inquiry into the State of Polite Learning'! That's what your 'Mind of the Race' means. Suppose one did it now, we should do it differently in every way from that."

"Yes, but how should we do it?" said I.

The project had laid hold upon me. I wanted a broad outline of the whole apparatus of thinking and determination in the modern State; something that should bring together all its various activities, which go on now in a sort of deliberate ignorance of one another, which would synthesize research, education, philosophical discussion, moral training, public policy. "There is," I said, "a disorganized abundance now."

"It's a sort of sub-conscious mind," said Boon, seeming to take me quite seriously, "with a half instinctive will." . . .

We discussed what would come into the book. One got an impression of the enormous range and volume of intellectual activity that pours along now, in comparison with the jejune trickle of Goldsmith's days. Then the world had—what? A few English writers, a few men in France, the Royal Society, the new Berlin Academy (conducting its transactions in French), all resting more or less upon the insecure patronage of the "Great"; a few schools, public and private, a couple of dozen of universities in all the world, a press of which *The Gentleman's Magazine* was the brightest ornament. Now——

It is a curious thing that it came to us both as a new effect, this enormously greater size of the intellectual world of to-day. We didn't at first grasp the implications of that difference, we simply found it necessitated an enlargement of our conception. "And then a man's thoughts lived too in a world that had been created, lock, stock, and barrel a trifle under six thousand years ago!" . . .

We fell to discussing the range and divisions of our subject. The main stream, we

THE MIND OF THE RACE

settled, was all that one calls "literature" in its broader sense. We should have to discuss that principally. But almost as important as the actual development of ideas, suggestions, ideals, is the way they are distributed through the body of humanity, developed, rendered, brought into touch with young minds and fresh minds, who are drawn so into participation, who themselves light up and become new thoughts. One had to consider journalism, libraries, book distribution, lecturing, teaching. Then there is the effect of laws, of inventions. . . . "Done in a large, dull, half-abstract way," said Boon, "one might fill volumes. One might become an Eminent Sociologist. You might even invent terminology. It's a chance——"

We let it pass. He went on almost at once to suggest a more congenial form, a conversational novel. I followed reluctantly. I share the general distrust of fiction as a vehicle of discussion. We would, he insisted, invent a personality who would embody our Idea, who should be fanatically obsessed by this idea of the Mind of the Race, who should preach it on all occasions and be brought into illuminating contact with all the existing mental apparatus and organization of the world. "Something of your deep moral earnestness, you know, only a little more presentable and not quite so vindictive," said Boon, "and without your—lapses. I seem to see him rather like Leo Maxse: the same white face, the same bright eyes, the same pervading suggestion of nervous intensity, the same earnest, quasi-reasonable voice—but instead of that anti-German obsession of his, an intelligent passion for the racial thought. He must be altogether a fanatic. He must think of the Mind of the Race in season and out of season. Collective thought will be no joke to him; it will be the supremely important thing. He will be passionately a patriot, entirely convinced of your proposition that 'the thought of a community is the life of a community,' and almost as certain that the tide of our thought is ebbing."

"Is it?" said I.

"I've never thought. The 'Encyclopædia Britannica' says it is."

"We must call the 'Encyclopædia Britannica.'"

"As a witness—in the book—rather! But, anyhow, this man of ours will believe it and struggle against it. It will make him ill; it will spoil the common things of life for him altogether. I seem to see him interrupting some nice, bright, clean English people at tennis. 'Look here, you know,' he will say, 'this is all very well. But have you *thought* to-day? They tell me the Germans are thinking, the Japanese.' I see him going in a sort of agony round and about Canterbury Cathedral. 'Here are all these beautiful, tranquil residences clustering round this supremely beautiful thing, all these well-dressed, excellent, fresh-coloured Englishmen in their beautiful clerical raiment—deans, canons—and what have they *thought,* any of them? I keep my ear to the *Hibbert Journal,* but is it enough?' Imagine him going through London on an omnibus. He will see as clear as the advertisements on the hoardings the signs of the formal breaking up of the old Victorian Church of England and Dissenting cultures that have held us together so long. He will see that the faith has gone, the habits no longer hold, the traditions lie lax like cut string— there is nothing to replace these things. People do this and that dispersedly; there is democracy in beliefs even, and any notion is as good as another. And there is America. Like a burst Haggis. Intellectually. The Mind is confused, the Race in the violent ferment of new ideas, in the explosive development of its own contrivances, has lost its head. It isn't thinking any more; it's stupefied one moment and the next it's diving about——

"It will be as clear as day to him that a great effort of intellectual self-control must come if the race is to be saved from utter confusion and dementia. And nobody seems to see it but he. He will go about wringing

THE MIND OF THE RACE

his hands, so to speak. I fancy him at last at a writing-desk, nervous white fingers clutched in his black hair. 'How can I put it so that they *must* attend and see?'"

So we settled on our method and principal character right away. But we got no farther because Boon insisted before doing anything else on drawing a fancy portrait of this leading character of ours and choosing his name. We decided to call him Hallery, and that he should look something like this—

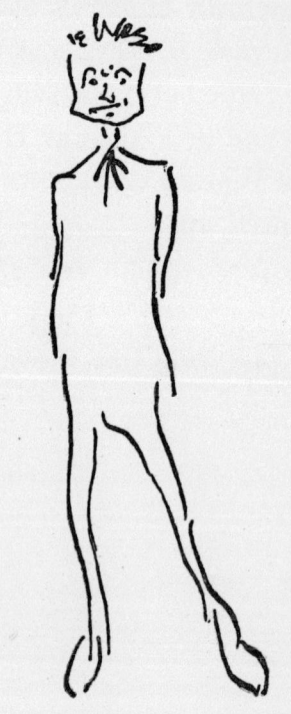

Hallery preparing to contradict.

That was how "The Mind of the Race" began, the book that was to have ended at last in grim burlesque with Hallery's murder of Dr. Tomlinson Keyhole in his villa at Hampstead, and the conversation at dawn with that incredulous but literate policeman at Highgate—he was reading a World's Classic—to whom Hallery gave himself up.

CHAPTER III

THE GREAT SLUMP, THE REVIVAL OF LETTERS, AND THE GARDEN BY THE SEA

1

THE story, as Boon planned it, was to begin with a spacious Introduction. We were to tell of the profound decadence of letters at the opening of the Twentieth Century and how a movement of revival began. A few notes in pencil of this opening do exist among the Remains, and to those I have referred. He read them over to me. . . .

" 'We begin,' " he said, " 'in a minor key. The impetus of the Romantic movement we declare is exhausted; the Race Mind, not only of the English-speaking peoples but of the whole world, has come upon a period of lethargy. The Giants of the Victorian age——' "

My eye discovered a familiar binding among the flower-pots. "You have been consulting the 'Encyclopædia Britannica,' " I said.

He admitted it without embarrassment.

"I have prigged the whole thing from the last Victorian Edition—with some slight variations. . . . 'The Giants of the Victorian age had passed. Men looked in vain for their successors. For a time there was an evident effort to fill the vacant thrones; for a time it seemed that the unstinted exertions of Miss Marie Corelli, Mr. Hall Caine, Mrs. Humphry Ward, and the friends of Mr. Stephen Phillips might go some way towards obliterating these magnificent gaps. And then, slowly but surely, it crept into men's minds that the game was up——' "

"You will alter that phrase?" I said.

"Certainly. But it must serve now . . . 'that, humanly speaking, it was impossible that anything, at once so large, so copious, so broadly and unhesitatingly popular, so nobly cumulative as the Great Victorian Reputations could ever exist again. The Race seemed threatened with intellectual barrenness; it had dropped its great blossoms, and stood amidst the pile of their wilting but still showy petals, budless and bare. It is curious to recall the public utterances upon literature that distinguished this desolate and melancholy time. It is a chorus of despair. There is in the comments of such admirable but ageing critics as still survived, of Mr. Gosse, for example, and the venerable Sir Sidney Colvin and Mr. Mumchance, an inevitable suggestion of widowhood; the judges, bishops, statesmen who are called to speak upon literature speak in the same reminiscent, inconsolable note as of a thing that is dead. Year after year one finds the speakers at the Dinner of the Royal Literary Fund admitting the impudence of their appeal. I remember at one of these festivities hearing the voice of Mr. Justice Gummidge break. . . . The strain, it is needless to say, found its echo in Dr. Tomlinson Keyhole; he confessed he never read anything that is less than thirty years old with the slightest enjoyment, and threw out the suggestion that nothing new should be published—at least for a considerable time—unless it was clearly shown to be posthumous. . . .

"'Except for a few irresistible volumes of facetiousness, the reading public very obediently followed the indications of authority in these matters, just as it had followed authority and sustained the Giants in the great Victorian days. It bought the long-neglected classics—anything was adjudged a classic that was out of copyright—it did its best to read them, to find a rare smack in their faded allusions, an immediate application for their forgotten topics. It made believe that architects were still like Mr. Pecksniff and schoolmasters like Squeers, that there were no different women from Jane Austen's women, and that social wisdom ended in Ruskin's fine disorder. But with the decay of any intellectual observation of the present these past things had lost their vitality. A few resolute people maintained an artificial interest in them by participation in quotation-hunting competitions and the like, but the great bulk of the educated classes ceased presently to read anything whatever. The classics were still bought by habit, as people who have lost faith will still go to church; but it is only necessary to examine some surviving volume of this period to mark the coruscation of printer's errors, the sheets bound in upside down or accidentally not inked in printing or transferred from some sister classic in the same series, to realize that these volumes were mere receipts for the tribute paid by the pockets of stupidity to the ancient prestige of thought. . . .

"'An air of completion rested upon the whole world of letters. A movement led by Professor Armstrong, the eminent educationist, had even gone some way towards banishing books from the schoolroom—their last refuge. People went about in the newly invented automobile and played open-air games;

THE GARDEN BY THE SEA

they diverted what attention they had once given to their minds to the more rational treatment of their stomachs. Reading became the last resort of those too sluggish or too poor to play games; one had recourse to it as a substitute for the ashes of more strenuous times in the earlier weeks of mourning for a near relative, and even the sale of classics began at last to decline. An altogether more satisfying and alluring occupation for the human intelligence was found in the game of Bridge. This was presently improved into Auction Bridge. Preparations were made for the erection of a richly decorative memorial in London to preserve the memory of Shakespeare, an English Taj Mahal; an Academy of uncreative literature was established under the Presidency of Lord Reay (who had never written anything at all), and it seemed but the matter of a few years before the goal of a complete and final mental quiet would be attained by the whole English-speaking community. . . .'"

2

"YOU know," I said, "that doesn't exactly represent——"

"Hush!" said Boon. "It was but a resting phase! And at this point I part company with the 'Encyclopædia.'"

"But you didn't get all that out of the 'Encyclopædia'?"

"Practically—yes. I may have rearranged it a little. The Encyclopædist is a most interesting and representative person. He takes up an almost eighteenth-century attitude, holds out hopes of a revival of Taste under an Academy, declares the interest of the great mass of men in literature is always 'empirical,' regards the great Victorian boom in letters as quite abnormal, and seems to ignore what you would call that necessary element of vitalizing thought. . . . It's just here that Hallery will have to dispute with him. We shall have to bring them together in our book somehow. . . . Into this impressive scene of decline and the ebb of all thinking comes this fanatic Hallery of ours, reciting with passionate conviction, 'the thought of a nation is the life of a nation.' You see our leading effect?"

He paused. "We have to represent Hallery as a voice crying in the wilderness. We have to present him in a scene of infinite intellectual bleakness, with the thinnest scrub of second-rate books growing contemptibly, and patches of what the Encyclopædist calls tares—wind-wilted tares—about him. A mournful Encyclopædist like some lone bird circling in the empty air beneath the fading stars. . . . Well, something of that effect, anyhow! And then, you know, suddenly, mysteriously one grows aware of light, of something coming, of something definitely coming, of the dawn of a great Literary Revival." . . .

"How does it come?"

"Oh! In the promiscuous way of these

things. The swing of the pendulum, it may be. Some eminent person gets bored at the prospect of repeating that rigmarole about the great Victorians and our present slackness for all the rest of his life, and takes a leaf from one of Hallery's books. We might have something after the fashion of the Efficiency and Wake-up England affair. Have you ever heard guinea-fowl at dawn?"

"I've heard them at twilight. They say, 'Come back. Come back.' But what has that to do with——"

"Nothing. There's a movement, a stir, a twittering, and then a sudden promiscuous uproar, articles in the reviews, articles in the newspapers, paragraphs, letters, associations, societies, leagues. I imagine a very great personality indeed in the most extraordinary and unexpected way coming in. . . ." (It was one of Boon's less amiable habits to impute strange and uncanny enterprises, the sudden adoption of movements, manias, propagandas, adhesion to vegetarianism, socialism, the strangest eccentricities, to the British royal family.) "As a result Hallery finds himself perforce a person of importance. 'The thought of a nation is the life of a nation,' one hears it from royal lips; 'a literature, a living soul, adequate to this vast empire,' turns up in the speech of a statesman of the greatest literary pretensions. Arnold White responds to the new note. The *Daily Express* starts a Literary Revival on its magazine page and offers a prize. The *Times* follows suit. Reports of what is afoot reach social circles in New York. . . . The illumination passes with a dawnlike swiftness right across the broad expanse of British life, east and west flash together; the ladies' papers and the motoring journals devote whole pages to 'New Literature,' and there is an enormous revival of Book Teas. . . . That sort of thing, you know—extensively."

3

"SO much by way of prelude. Now picture to yourself the immediate setting of my conference. Just hand me that book by the 'Encyclopædia.'"

It was Mallock's "New Republic." He took it, turned a page or so, stuck a finger in it, and resumed.

"It is in a narrow, ill-kept road by the seaside, Bliss. A long wall, plaster-faced, blotched and peeling, crested with uncivil glass against the lower orders, is pierced by cast-iron gates clumsily classical, and through the iron bars of these there is visible the deserted gatekeeper's lodge, its cracked windows opaque with immemorial dirt, and a rich undergrowth of nettles beneath the rusty cypresses and stone pines that border the carriage-way. An automobile throbs in the road; its occupants regard a board leaning all askew above the parapet, and hesitate to descend.

On the board, which has been enriched by the attentions of the passing boy with innumerable radiant mud pellets, one reads with difficulty—

THIS CLASSICAL VILLA

with magnificent gardens in the Victorian-Italian style reaching down to the sea, and replete with Latin and Greek inscriptions, a garden study, literary associations, fully matured Oxford allusions, and a great number of conveniently arranged bedrooms, to be

LET OR SOLD.

Apply to the owner,
Mr. W. H. MALLOCK,

original author of
"The New Republic."

Key within.

"'This *must* be it, my dear Archer,' says one of the occupants of the motor-car, and he rises, throws aside his furs, and reveals—the urbane presence of the Encyclopædist. He descends, and rings a clangorous bell. . . . Eh?"

"It's the garden of the 'New Republic'?"

"Exactly. Revisited. It's an astonishing thing. Do you know the date of the 'New Republic'? The book's nearly forty years old! About the time of Matthew Arnold's 'Friendship's Garland,' and since that time there's been nothing like a systematic stock-taking of the English-speaking mind—until the Encyclopædist reported 'no effects.' And I propose to make this little party in the motor-car a sort of scratch expedition, under the impetus of the proposed Revival of Thought. They are prospecting for a Summer Congress, which is to go into the state of the republic of letters thoroughly. It isn't perhaps quite Gosse's style, but he has to be there—in a way he's the official British man of letters—but we shall do what we can for him, we shall make him show a strong disposition towards protective ironies and confess himself not a little bothered at being dragged into the horrid business. And I think we must have George Moore, who has played uncle to so many movements and been so uniformly disappointed in his nephews. And William Archer, with that face of his which is so exactly like his mind, a remarkably fine face mysteriously marred by an expression of unscrupulous integrity. And lastly, Keyhole."

"Why Keyhole?" I asked.

"Hallery has to murder some one. I've planned that—and who *would* he murder but Keyhole? . . . And we have to hold the first meeting in Mallock's garden to preserve the continuity of English thought.

"Very well! Then we invent a morose, elderly caretaker, greatly embittered at this irruption. He parleys for a time through the gate with all the loyalty of his class, mentions a number of discouraging defects, more particularly in the drainage, alleges the whole place is clammy, and only at Gosse's clearly enunciated determination to enter produces the key."

Boon consulted his text. "Naturally one would give a chapter to the Villa by the Sea and Mallock generally. Our visitors explore. They visit one scene after another familiar to the good Mallockite; they descend 'the broad flights of steps flanked by Gods and Goddesses' that lead from one to another of the 'long, straight terraces set with vases and Irish yews,' and the yews, you know, have suffered from the want of water, the vases are empty, and ivy, under the benediction of our modest climate, has already veiled the classical freedom—the conscientious nudity, one might say—of the statuary. The laurels have either grown inordinately or perished, and the 'busts of orators, poets, and philosophers' 'with Latin inscriptions,' stand either bleakly exposed or else swallowed up in a thicket. There is a pleasing struggle to translate the legends, and one gathers scholarship is not extinct in England.

"The one oasis in a universal weediness is the pond about the 'scaly Triton,' which has been devoted to the culture of spring onions, a vegetable to which the aged custodian quite superfluously avows himself very 'partial.' The visitors return to the house, walk along its terrace, survey its shuttered front, and they spend some time going through its musty rooms. Dr. Keyhole distinguishes himself by the feverish eagerness of his curiosity about where Leslie slept and where was the boudoir of Mrs. Sinclair. He insists that a very sad and painful scandal about these two underlies the *New Republic,* and professes a thirsty desire to draw a veil over it as conspicuously as possible. The others drag him away to the summer dining-room, now a great brier tangle, where once Lady Grace so pleasantly dined her guests. The little arena about the fountain in a porphyry basin they do not find, but the garden study they peer into, and see its inkpot in the shape of a classical temple, just as Mr. Mallock has described it, and the windowless theatre, and, in addition, they find a small private gas-works that served it. The old man lets them in, and by the light of uplifted vestas they see the decaying, rat-disordered ruins of the scene before which Jenkinson who was Jowett, and Herbert who was Ruskin, preached. It is as like a gorge in the Indian Caucasus as need be. The Brocken act-drop above hangs low enough to show the toes of the young witch, still brightly pink. . . .

"They go down to the beach, and the old man, with evil chuckles, recalls a hitherto unpublished anecdote of mixed bathing in the 'seventies, in which Mrs. Sinclair and a flushed and startled Dr. Jenkinson, Greek in thought rather than action, play the chief parts, and then they wade through a nettle-bed to that 'small classical portico' which leads to the locked enclosure containing the three tombs, with effigies after the fashion of Genoa Cemetery. But the key of the gate is lost, so that they cannot go in to examine them, and the weeds have hidden the figures altogether.

" 'That's a pity,' some one remarks, 'for it's here, no doubt, that old Laurence lies, with his first mistress and his last—under these cypresses.'

"The aged custodian makes a derisive noise, and every one turns to him.

" 'I gather you throw some doubt?' the Encyclopædist begins in his urbane way.

" 'Buried—under the cypresses—first mistress and last!' The old man makes his manner invincibly suggestive of scornful merriment.

" 'But isn't it so?'

" 'Bless y'r 'art, *no!* Mr. Laurence—buried! Mr. Laurence worn't never alive!'

" 'But there was a *young* Mr. Laurence?'

" 'That was Mr. Mallup 'imself, that was! 'E was a great mistifier was Mr. Mallup, and sometimes 'e went about pretendin' to be Mr. Laurence and sometimes he was Mr. Leslie, and sometimes—— But there, you'd 'ardly believe. 'E got all this up—cypresses, chumes, everythink—out of 'is 'ed.

Po'try. Why! 'Ere! Jest come along 'ere, gents!'

"He leads the way along a narrow privet alley that winds its surreptitious way towards an alcove.

" 'Miss Merton,' he says, flinging the door of this open.

" 'The Roman Catholic young person?' says Dr. Tomlinson Keyhole.

" 'Quite right, sir,' says the aged custodian.

"They peer in.

"Hanging from a peg the four visitors behold a pale blue dress cut in the fashion of the 'seventies, a copious 'chignon' of fair hair, large earrings, and on the marble bench a pair of open-work stockings and other articles of feminine apparel. A tall mirror hangs opposite these garments, and in a little recess convenient to the hand are the dusty and decaying materials for a hasty 'make-up.'

"The old custodian watches the effect of this display upon the others with masked enjoyment.

" 'You mean Miss Merton *painted?*' said the Encyclopædist, knitting his brows.

" 'Mr. Mallup did,' says the aged custodian.

" 'You mean——?'

" 'Mr. Mallup was Miss Merton. 'E got 'er up too. Parst 'er orf as a young lady, 'e did. Oh, 'e was a great mistifier was Mr. Mallup. None of the three of 'em wasn't real people, really; he got 'em all up.'

" 'She had sad-looking eyes, a delicate, proud mouth, and a worn, melancholy look,' muses Mr. Archer.

" 'And young Laurence was in love with her,' adds the Encyclopædist. . . .

" 'They was all Mr. Mallup,' says the aged custodian. 'Made up out of 'is 'ed. And the gents that pretended they was Mr. 'Uxley and Mr. Tyndall in disguise, one was Bill Smithers, the chemist's assistant, and the other was the chap that used to write and print the *Margate Advertiser* before the noo papers come.' "

CHAPTER IV

OF ART, OF LITERATURE, OF MR. HENRY JAMES

1

THE Garden by the Sea chapter was to have gone on discursively with a discussion upon this project of a conference upon the Mind of the Race. The automobileful of gentlemen who had first arrived was to have supplied the opening interlocutors, but presently they were to have been supplemented by the most unexpected accessories. It would have been an enormously big dialogue if it had ever been written, and Boon's essentially lazy temperament was all against its ever getting written. There were to have been disputes from the outset as to the very purpose that had brought them all together. "A sort of literary stock-taking" was to have been Mr. Archer's phrase. Repeated. Unhappily, its commercialism was to upset Mr. Gosse extremely; he was to say something passionately bitter about its "utter lack of dignity." Then relenting a little, he was to urge as an alternative "some controlling influence, some standard and restraint, a new and better Academic influence." Dr. Keyhole was to offer his journalistic services in organizing an Academic plebiscite, a suggestion which was to have exasperated Mr. Gosse to the pitch of a gleaming silence.

In the midst of this conversation the party is joined by Hallery and an American friend, a quiet Harvard sort of man speaking meticulously accurate English, and still later by emissaries of Lord Northcliffe and Mr. Hearst, by Mr. Henry James, rather led into it by a distinguished hostess, by Mr. W. B. Yeats, late but keen, and by that Sir Henry Lunn who organizes the Swiss winter sports hotels. All these people drift in with an all too manifestly simulated accidentalness that at last arouses the distrust of the elderly custodian, so that Mr. Orage, the gifted editor of the *New Age,* arriving last, is refused admission. The sounds of the conflict at the gates do but faintly perturb the conference within, which is now really getting to business, but afterwards Mr. Orage, slightly wounded in the face by a dexterously plied rake and incurably embittered, makes his existence felt by a number of unpleasant missiles discharged from over the wall in the direction of any audible voices. Ultimately Mr. Orage gets into a point of vantage in a small pine-tree overlooking the seaward corner of the premises, and from this he contributes a number of comments that are rarely helpful, always unamiable, and frequently in the worst possible taste.

Such was Boon's plan for the second chapter of "The Mind of the Race." But that chapter he never completely planned. At various times Boon gave us a number of colloquies, never joining them together in any regular order. The project of taking up the discussion of the Mind of the Race at the exact point Mr. Mallock had laid it down, and taking the villa by the sea for the meeting-place, was at once opposed by Hallery and his American friend with an evidently preconcerted readiness. They pointed out the entire democratization of thought and literature that had been going on for the past four decades. It was no longer possible to deal with such matters in the old aristocratic country-house style; it was no longer possible to take them up from that sort of beginning; the centre of mental gravity among the English-speaking community had shifted socially and geographically; what was needed now was something wider and ampler, something more in the nature of such a conference as the annual meeting of the British Association. Science left the gentleman's mansion long ago; literature must follow it—had followed it. To come back to Mr. Lankester's Villa by the sea was to come back to a beaten covert. The Hearst representative took up a strongly supporting position, and suggested that if indeed we wished to move with the times the thing to do was to strike out boldly for a special annex of the Panama Exhibition at San Francisco and for organization upon sound American lines. It was a case, he said, even for "exhibits." Sir Henry Lunn, however, objected that in America the Anglo-Saxon note was almost certain to be too exclusively sounded; that we had to remember there were vigorous cultures growing up and growing up more and more detachedly upon the continent of Europe; we wanted, at least, their reflected lights . . . some more central position. . . . In fact, Switzerland . . . where also numerous convenient hotels . . . patronized, he gathered from the illustrated papers, by Lord Lytton, Mrs. Asquith, Mr. F. R. Benson . . . and all sorts of helpful leading people.

2

MEANWHILE Boon's plan was to make Mr. George Moore and Mr. Henry James wander off from the general dispute, and he invented a dialogue that even at the time struck me as improbable, in which both gentlemen pursue entirely independent trains of thought.

Mr. Moore's conception of the projected symposium was something rather in the vein of the journeyings of Shelley, Byron, and their charming companions through France to Italy, but magnified to the dimensions of an enormous pilgrimage, enlarged to the scale of a stream of refugees. "What, my dear James," he asked, "is this mind of humanity at all without a certain touch of romance, of adventure? Even Mallock appreciated the significance of *frou-frou;* but these fellows behind here . . ."

To illustrate his meaning better, he was to

have told, with an extraordinary and loving mastery of detail, of a glowing little experience that had been almost forced upon him at Nismes by a pretty little woman from Nebraska, and the peculiar effect it had had, and particularly the peculiar effect that the coincidence that both Nebraska and Nismes begin with an "N" and end so very differently, had had upon his imagination. . . .

Meanwhile Mr. James, being anxious not merely to state but also to ignore, laboured through the long cadences of his companion as an indefatigable steam-tug might labour endlessly against a rolling sea, elaborating his own particular point about the proposed conference.

"Owing it as we do," he said, "very, very largely to our friend Gosse, to that peculiar, that honest but restless and, as it were, at times almost malignantly ambitious organizing energy of our friend, I cannot altogether —altogether, even if in any case I should have taken so extreme, so devastatingly isolating a step as, to put it violently, *stand out;* yet I must confess to a considerable anxiety, a kind of distress, an apprehension, the terror, so to speak, of the kerbstone, at all this stream of intellectual trafficking, of going to and fro, in a superb and towering manner enough no doubt, but still essentially going to and fro rather than in any of the completed senses of the word *getting there,* that does so largely constitute the aggregations and activities we are invited to traverse. My poor head, such as it is and as much as it can and upon such legs—save the mark!—as it can claim, must, I suppose, play its inconsiderable part among the wheels and the rearings and the toots and the whistles and all this uproar, this—Mm, Mm!—let us say, this *infernal* uproar, of the occasion; and if at times one has one's doubts before plunging in, whether after all, after the plunging and the dodging and the close shaves and narrow squeaks, one does begin to feel that one is getting through, whether after all one *will* get through, and whether indeed there is any getting through, whether, to deepen and enlarge and display one's doubt quite openly, there is in truth any sort of ostensible and recognizable other side attainable and definable at all, whether to put this thing with a lucidity that verges on the brutal, whether our amiable and in most respects our adorable Gosse isn't indeed preparing here and now, not the gathering together of a conference but the assembling, the *meet,* so to speak, of a wild-goose chase of an entirely desperate and hopeless description."

At that moment Mr. George Moore was saying: "Little exquisite shoulders without a touch of colour and with just that suggestion of rare old ivory in an old shop window in some out-of-the-way corner of Paris that only the most patent abstinence from baths and the brutality of soaping——"

Each gentleman stopped simultaneously.

Ahead the path led between box-hedges to a wall, and above the wall was a pine-tree, and the Editor of the *New Age* was reascending the pine-tree in a laborious and resolute manner, gripping with some difficulty in his hand a large and very formidable lump of unpleasantness. . . .

With a common impulse the two gentlemen turned back towards the house.

Mr. James was the first to break the momentary silence. "And so, my dear Moore, and so—to put it shortly—without any sort of positive engagement or entanglement or pledge or pressure—I *came*. And at the proper time and again with an entirely individual detachment and as little implication as possible I shall *go*." . . .

Subsequently Mr. James was to have buttonholed Hallery's American, and in the warm bath of his sympathy to have opened and bled slowly from another vein of thought.

"I admit the abundance of—what shall I say?—*activities* that our friend is summoning, the tremendous wealth of matter, of material for literature and art, that has accumulated during the last few decades. No one could appreciate, could savour and watch and respond, more than myself to the tremendous growing clangour of the mental process as the last half-century has exhibited it. But when it comes to the enterprise of gathering it together, and not simply just gathering it together, but gathering it *all* together, then surely one must at some stage ask the question, *Why* all? Why, in short, attempt to a comprehensiveness that must be overwhelming when in fact the need is for a selection that shall not merely represent but elucidate and lead. Aren't we, after all, all of us after some such indicating projection of a leading digit, after such an insistence on the outstandingly essential in face of this abundance, this saturation, this fluid chaos that perpetually increases? Here we are gathering together to celebrate and summarize literature in some sort of undefined and unprecedented fashion, and for the life of me I find it impossible to determine what among my numerous associates and friends and—to embrace still larger quantities of the stuff in hand—my contemporaries is considered to be the literature in question. So confused now are we between matter and treatment, between what is stated and documented and what is prepared and presented, that for the life of me I do not yet see whether we are supposed to be building an ark or whether by immersion and the meekest of submersions and an altogether complete submission of our distended and quite helpless carcasses to its incalculable caprice we are supposed to be celebrating and, in the whirling uncomfortable fashion of flotsam at large, indicating and making visible the whole tremendous cosmic inundation." . . .

Mr. James converses with Mr. George Moore upon matters of vital importance to both of them.

3

IT was entirely in the quality of Boon's intellectual untidiness that for a time he should go off at a tangent in pursuit of Mr. Henry James and leave his literary picnic disseminated about the grounds of Mr. Mallock's villa. There, indeed, they remained. The story when he took it up again picked up at quite a different point.

I remember how Boon sat on the wall of his vegetable garden and discoursed upon James, while several of us squatted about on the cucumber-frames and big flowerpots and suchlike seats, and how over the wall Ford Madox Hueffer was beating Wilkins at Badminton. Hueffer wanted to come and talk too; James is one of his countless subjects—and what an omniscient man he is too!—but Wilkins was too cross to let him off. . . .

So that all that Hueffer was able to contribute was an exhortation not to forget that

Henry James knew Turgenev and that he had known them both, and a flat denial that Dickens was a novelist. This last was the tail of that Pre-Raphaelite feud begun in *Household Words,* oh! generations ago. . . .

"Got you there, my boy!" said Wilkins. "Seven, twelve."

We heard no more from Hueffer.

"You see," Boon said, "you can't now talk of literature without going through James. James is unavoidable. James is to criticism what Immanuel Kant is to philosophy—a partially comprehensible essential, an inevitable introduction. If you understand what James is up to and if you understand what James is not up to, then you are placed. You are in the middle of the critical arena. You are in a position to lay about you with significance. Otherwise. . . .

"I want to get this Hallery of mine, who is to be the hero of 'The Mind of the Race,' into a discussion with Henry James, but that, you know, is easier said than imagined. Hallery is to be one of those enthusiastic thinkers who emit highly concentrated opinion in gobbets, suddenly. James—isn't." . . .

Boon meditated upon his difficulties. "Hallery's idea of literature is something tremendously comprehensive, something that pierces always down towards the core of things, something that carries and changes all the activities of the race. This sort of thing."

He read from a scrap of paper—

" 'The thought of a community is the life of that community, and if the collective thought of a community is disconnected and fragmentary, then the community is collectively vain and weak. That does not constitute an incidental defect but essential failure. Though that community have cities such as the world has never seen before, fleets and hosts and glories, though it count its soldiers by the army corps and its children by the million, yet if it hold not to the reality of thought and formulated will beneath these outward things, it will pass, and all its glories will pass, like smoke before the wind, like mist beneath the sun; it will become at last only one more vague and fading dream upon the scroll of time, a heap of mounds and pointless history, even as are Babylon and Nineveh.'"

"I've heard that before somewhere," said Dodd.

"Most of this dialogue will have to be quotation," said Boon.

"He makes literature include philosophy?"

"Everything. It's all the central things. It's the larger Bible to him, a thing about which all the conscious direction of life revolves. It's alive with passion and will. Or if it isn't, then it ought to be. . . . And then as the antagonist comes this artist, this man who seems to regard the whole seething brew of life as a vat from which you skim, with slow, dignified gestures, works of art. . . . Works of art whose only claim is their art. . . . Hallery is going to be very impatient about art."

"Ought there to be such a thing as a literary artist?" some one said.

"Ought there, in fact, to be Henry James?" said Dodd.

"I don't think so. Hallery won't think so. You see, the discussion will be very fundamental. There's contributory art, of course, and a way of doing things better or worse. Just as there is in war, or cooking. But the way of doing isn't the end. First the end must be judged—and then if you like talk of how it is done. Get there as splendidly as possible. But get there. James and George Moore, neither of them take it like that. They leave out getting there, or the thing they get to is so trivial as to amount to scarcely more than an omission." . . .

Boon reflected. "In early life both these men poisoned their minds in studios. Thought about pictures even might be less studio-ridden than it is. But James has never discovered that a novel isn't a picture. . . . That life isn't a studio. . . .

"He wants a novel to be simply and completely *done*. He wants it to have a unity, he demands homogeneity. . . . Why *should* a book have that? For a picture it's reasonable, because you have to see it all at once. But there's no need to see a book all at once. It's like wanting to have a whole county done in one style and period of architecture. It's like insisting that a walking tour must stick to one valley. . . .

"But James *begins* by taking it for granted that a novel is a work of art that must be judged by its oneness. Judged first by its oneness. Some one gave him that idea in the beginning of things and he has never found it out. He doesn't find things out. He doesn't even seem to want to find things out. You can see that in him; he is eager to accept things —elaborately. You can see from his books that he accepts etiquettes, precedences, associations, claims. That is his peculiarity. He accepts very readily and then—elaborates. He has, I am convinced, one of the strongest, most abundant minds alive in the whole world, and he has the smallest penetration. Indeed, he has no penetration. He is the culmination of the Superficial type. Or else he would have gone into philosophy and been greater even than his wonderful brother. . . . But here he is, spinning about, like the most tremendous of water boatmen—you know those insects?—kept up by surface tension. As if, when once he pierced the surface, he would drown. It's incredible. A water boatman as big as an elephant. I was reading him only yesterday 'The Golden Bowl'; it's dazzling how never for a moment does he go through."

"Recently he's been explaining himself," said Dodd.

"His 'Notes on Novelists.' It's one sustained demand for the picture effect. Which is the denial of the sweet complexity of life, of the pointing this way and that, of the spider on the throne. Philosophy aims at a unity and never gets there. . . . That true unity which we all suspect, and which no one attains, if it is to be got at all it is to be got by penetrating, penetrating down and through. The picture, on the other hand, is forced to a unity because it can see only one aspect at a time. I am doubtful even about that. Think of Hogarth or Carpaccio. But if the novel is to follow life it must be various and discursive. Life is diversity and entertainment, not completeness and satisfaction. All actions are half-hearted, shot delightfully with wandering thoughts—about something else. All true stories are a felt of irrelevances. But James sets out to make his novels with the presupposition that they can be made continuously relevant. And perceiving the discordant things, he tries to get rid of them. He sets himself to pick the straws out of the hair of Life before he paints her. But without the straws she is no longer the mad woman we love. He talks of 'selection,' and of making all of a novel definitely *about* a theme. He objects to a 'saturation' that isn't oriented. And he objects, if you go into it, for no clear reason at all. Following up his conception of selection, see what in his own practice he omits. In practice James's selection becomes just omission and nothing more. He omits everything that demands digressive treatment or collateral statement. For example, he omits opinions. In all his novels you will find no people with defined political opinions, no people with religious opinions, none with clear partisanships or with lusts or whims, none definitely up to any specific impersonal thing. There are no poor people dominated by the imperatives of Saturday night and Monday morning, no dreaming types—and don't we all more or less live dreaming? And none are ever decently forgetful. All that much of humanity he clears out before he begins his story. It's like cleaning rabbits for the table.

"But you see how relentlessly it follows from the supposition that the novel is a work of art aiming at pictorial unities!

"All art too acutely self-centred comes to

this sort of thing. James's denatured people are only the equivalent in fiction of those egg-faced, black-haired ladies, who sit and sit, in the Japanese colour-prints, the unresisting stuff for an arrangement of blacks. . . .

"Then with the eviscerated people he has invented he begins to make up stories. What stories they are! Concentrated on suspicion, on a gift, on possessing a 'piece' of old furniture, on what a little girl may or may not have noted in an emotional situation. These people cleared for artistic treatment never make lusty love, never go to angry war, never shout at an election or perspire at poker; never in any way *date*. . . . And upon the petty residuum of human interest left to them they focus minds of a Jamesian calibre. . . .

"The only living human motives left in the novels of Henry James are a certain avidity and an entirely superficial curiosity. Even when relations are irregular or when sins are hinted at, you feel that these are merely attitudes taken up, gambits before the game of

attainment and over-perception begins. . . .
His people nose out suspicions, hint by hint,
link by link. Have you ever known living human beings do that? The thing his novel is
about is always there. It is like a church lit
but without a congregation to distract you,
with every light and line focused on the high
altar. And on the altar, very reverently
placed, intensely there, is a dead kitten, an
egg-shell, a bit of string. . . . Like his *Altar of the Dead,* with nothing to the dead at
all. . . . For if there was they couldn't all
be candles and the effect would vanish. . . .
And the elaborate, copious emptiness of the
whole Henry James exploit is only redeemed
and made endurable by the elaborate, copious wit. Upon the desert his selection has
made Henry James erects palatial metaphors.
. . . The chief fun, the only exercise, in
reading Henry James is this clambering over
vast metaphors. . . .

"Having first made sure that he has scarcely
anything left to express, he then sets to work

to express it, with an industry, a wealth of intellectual stuff that dwarfs Newton. He spares no resource in the telling of his dead inventions. He brings up every device of language to state and define. Bare verbs he rarely tolerates. He splits his infinitives and fills them up with adverbial stuffing. He presses the passing colloquialism into his service. His vast paragraphs sweat and struggle; they could not sweat and elbow and struggle more if God Himself was the processional meaning to which they sought to come. And all for tales of nothingness. . . . It is leviathan retrieving pebbles. It is a magnificent but painful hippopotamus resolved at any cost, even at the cost of its dignity, upon picking up a pea which has got into a corner of its den. Most things, it insists, are beyond it, but it can, at any rate, modestly, and with an artistic singleness of mind, pick up that pea." . . .

4

"A LITTLE while ago," said Boon, suddenly struggling with his trouser pocket and producing some pieces of paper, "I sketched out a novel, and as it was rather in the manner of Henry James I think perhaps you might be interested by it now. So much, that is, as there is of it. It is to be called 'The Spoils of Mr. Blandish,' and it is all about this particular business of the selective life. Mr. Blandish, as I saw him, was pretty completely taken from the James ideal. . . . He was a man with an exquisite apprehension of particulars, with just that sense of there being a rightness attainable, a fitness, a charm, a finish. . . . In any little affair. . . . He believed that in speech and still more that in writing there was an inevitable right word, in actions great and small a mellowed etiquette, in everything a possible perfection. He was, in fact, the very soul of

Henry James—as I understand it. . . . This sort of man—

Mr. Blandish going delicately through life. "Oh no! oh no! But Yes! and This is it!"

"Going delicately."

I was able to secure the sketch.

"He didn't marry, he didn't go upon adventures; lust, avarice, ambition, all these things that as Milton says are to be got 'not without dust and heat,' were not for him. Blood and dust and heat—he ruled them out.

But he had independent means, he could live freely and delicately and charmingly, he could travel and meet and be delighted by all the best sorts of people in the best sorts of places. So for years he enriched his resonances, as an admirable violin grows richer with every note it sounds. He went about elaborately, avoiding ugliness, death, suffering, industrialism, politics, sport, the thought of war, the red blaze of passion. He travelled widely in the more settled parts of the world. Chiefly he visited interesting and ancient places, putting his ever more exquisite sensorium at them, consciously taking delicate impressions upon the refined wax of his being. In a manner most carefully occasional, he wrote. Always of faded places. His 'Ypres' was wonderful. His 'Bruges' and his 'Hour of Van Eyk' . . .

"Such," said Boon, "is the hero. The story begins, oh! quite in the James manner with——" He read—

"'At times it seemed inaccessible, a thing beyond hope, beyond imagining, and then at times it became so concrete an imagination, a desire so specific, so nearly expressed, as to grow if not to the exact particulars of longitude and latitude, yet at any rate so far as county and district and atmosphere were concerned, so far indeed as an intuition of proximity was concerned, an intimation that made it seem at last at certain moments as if it could not possibly be very much farther than just round the corner or over the crest.' . . .

"But I've left a good bit of that to write up. In the book there will be pages and sheets of that sentence. The gist is that Mr. Blandish wants a house to live in and that he has an idea of the kind of house he wants. And the chapter, the long, unresting, progressing chapter, expands and expands; it never jumps you forward, it never lets you off, you can't skip and you can't escape, until there comes at last a culminating distension of statement in which you realize more and more clearly, until you realize it with the unforgettable certainty of a thing long fought for and won at last, that Mr. Blandish has actually come upon the house and with a vigour of decision as vivid as a flash of lightning in a wilderness of troubled clouds, as vivid indeed as the loud, sonorous bursting of a long blown bladder, has said *'This is it!'* On that *'This is it'* my chapter ends, with an effect of enormous relief, with something of the beautiful serenity that follows a difficult parturition.

"The story is born.

"And then we leap forward to possession.

" 'And here he was, in the warmest reality, in the very heart of the materialization of his dream——' He has, in fact, got the house. For a year or so from its first accidental discovery he had done nothing but just covet the house; too fearful of an overwhelming disappointment even to make a definite inquiry as to its accessibility. But he has, you will gather, taken apartments in the neighbourhood, thither he visits frequently, and almost every day when he walks abroad the coveted house draws him. It is in a little seaside place on the east coast, and the only available walks are along the shore or inland across the golf-links. Either path offers tempting digressions towards *it*. He comes to know it from a hundred aspects and under a thousand conditions of light and atmosphere. . . . And while still in the early stage he began a curious and delicious secret practice in relationship. You have heard of the Spaniard in love, in love with a woman he had seen but once, whom he might never see again, a princess, etiquette-defended, a goddess, and who yet, seeing a necklace that became her, bought it for the joy of owning something that was at least by fitness hers. Even so did Mr. Blandish begin to buy first one little article and then, the fancy growing upon him more and more, things, 'pieces' they call them, that were in the vein of Samphire House. And then came the day, the wonderful day, when as he took his afternoon feast of the eye, the door opened, some one came out towards him. . . .

OF ART AND LITERATURE

"It was incredible. They were giving him tea with hot, inadvisable scones—but their hotness, their close heaviness, he accepted with a ready devotion, would have accepted had they been ten times as hot and close and heavy, not heedlessly, indeed, but gratefully, willingly paying his price for these astonishing revelations that without an effort, serenely, calmly, dropped in between her gentle demands whether he would have milk and her mild inquiries as to the exact quantity of sugar his habits and hygienic outlook demanded, that his hostess so casually made. These generous, heedless people were talking of departures, of abandonments, of, so they put it, selling the dear old place, if indeed any one could be found to buy a place so old and so remote and—she pointed her intention with a laugh—so very, very dear. Repletion of scones were a small price to pay for such a glowing, such an incredible gift of opportunity, thrust thus straight into the willing, amazed hands. . . .

"He gets the house. He has it done up. He furnishes it, and every article of furniture seems a stroke of luck too good to be true. And to crown it all I am going to write one of those long crescendo passages that James loves, a sentence, pages of it, of happy event linking to happy event until at last the incredible completion, a butler, unquestionably Early Georgian, respectability, competence equally unquestionable, a wife who could cook, and cook well, no children, no thought or possibility of children, and to crown all, the perfect name—Mutimer!

Mutimer at first.

"All this you must understand is told retrospectively as Blandish installs himself in Samphire House. It is told to the refrain, 'Still, fresh every morning, came the persuasion "This is too good to be true."' And as it is told, something else, by the most imperceptible degrees, by a gathering up of hints and allusions and pointing details, gets itself told too, and that is the growing realization in the mind of Blandish of a something extra, of something not quite bargained for,—the hoard and the haunting. About the house hangs a presence. . . .

"He had taken it at first as a mere picturesque accessory to the whole picturesque and delightful wreathing of association and tradition about the place, that there should be this ancient flavour of the cutlass and the keg, this faint aroma of buried doubloons and Stevensonian experiences. He had assumed, etc. . . . He had gathered, etc. . . . And it was in the most imperceptible manner that beyond his sense of these takings and assumptions and gatherings there grew his perception that the delicate quiver of appreciation, at first his utmost tribute to these illegal and adventurous and sanguinary associations, was broadening and strengthening, was, one hardly knew whether to say developing or degenerating, into a nervous reaction, more spinal and less equivocally agreeable, into the question, sensed rather than actually thought or asked, whether in fact the place didn't in certain lights and certain aspects and at certain unfavourable moments come near to evoking the ghost—if such sorites are permissible in the world of delicate shades—of the ghost, of the ghost of a shiver—of *aversion*. . . .

"And so at page a hundred and fifty or thereabouts we begin to get into the story," said Boon.

"You wade through endless marshes of subtle intimation, to a sense of a Presence in Samphire House. For a number of pages you are quite unable to tell whether this is a ghost or a legend or a foreboding or simply old-fashioned dreams that are being allusively placed before you. But there is an effect piled up very wonderfully, of Mr. Blandish, obsessed, uneasy, watching furtively and steadfastly his guests, his callers, his domestics, continually asking himself, 'Do they note it? Are they feeling it?'

"We break at last into incidents. A young friend of the impossible name of Deshman helps evolve the story; he comes to stay; he seems to feel the influence from the outset, he cannot sleep, he wanders about the house. . . . Do others know? *Others?* . . . The gardener takes to revisiting the gardens after nightfall. He is met in the shrubbery with an unaccountable spade in his hand and answers huskily. Why should a gardener carry a spade? Why should he answer huskily? Why should the presence, the doubt, the sense of something else elusively in the air about them, become intensified at the encounter? Oh! conceivably of course in many places, but just *there!* As some sort of protection, it may be. . . . Then suddenly as Mr. Blandish sits at his lonely but beautifully served dinner he becomes aware for the first time of a change in Mutimer.

Mutimer at the end of a year.

"Something told him in that instant that Mutimer also *knew*. . . .

"Deshman comes again with a new and disconcerting habit of tapping the panelling and measuring the thickness of the walls when he thinks no one is looking, and then a sister of Mr. Blandish and a friend, a woman, yet not so much a woman as a disembodied intelligence in a feminine costume with one of those impalpable relationships with Deshman that people have with one another in the world of Henry James, an association of shadows, an atmospheric liaison. Follow some almost sentenceless conversations. Mr. Blandish walks about the shrubbery with the friend, elaborately getting at it—whatever it is—and in front of them, now hidden by the yew hedges, now fully in view, walks Deshman with the married and settled sister of Mr. Blandish. . . .

" 'So,' said Mr. Blandish, pressing the point down towards the newly discovered sensitiveness, 'where we feel, he it seems *knows.*'

"She seemed to consider.

" 'He doesn't know completely,' was her qualification.

" 'But he has something—something, tangible.'

" 'If he can make it tangible.'

"On that the mind of Mr. Blandish played for a time.

" 'Then it isn't altogether tangible yet?'

" 'It isn't tangible enough for him to go upon.'

" 'Definitely something.'

"Her assent was mutely concise.

" 'That we on our part——?'

"The *we* seemed to trouble her.

" 'He knows more than you do,' she yielded.

"The gesture, the half turn, the momentary halt in the paces of Mr. Blandish, plied her further.

" 'More, I think, than he has admitted—to any one.'

" 'Even to you?'

"He perceived an interesting wave of irritation. 'Even to me,' he had wrung from her but at the price of all further discussion.

"Putting the thing crassly," said Boon, "Deshman has got wind of a hoard, of a treasure, of something—Heaven as yet only knows what something—buried, imbedded, in some as yet unexplained way incorporated with Samphire House. On the whole the stress lies rather on treasure, the treasure of smuggling, of longshore practices, of illegality on the high seas. And still clearer is it that the amiable Deshman wants to get at it without the participation of Mr. Blandish. Until the very end you are never quite satisfied why Deshman wants to get at it in so private a fashion. As the plot thickens you are played about between the conviction that Deshman wants the stuff for himself and the firm belief of the lady that against the possible intervention of the Treasury, he wants to secure it for Mr. Blandish, to secure it at least generously if nefariously, lest perhaps it should fall under the accepted definition and all the consequent confiscations of treasure trove. And there are further beautiful subtleties as to whether she really believes in this more kindly interpretation of the refined but dubitable Deshman. . . . A friend of Deshman's, shameless under the incredible name of Mimbleton, becomes entangled in this thick, sweet flow of narrative—the James method of introducing a character always reminds me of going round with the lantern when one is treacling for moths. Mimbleton has energy. He presses. Under a summer dawn of delicious sweetness Mimbleton is found insensible on the croquet lawn by Mr. Blandish, who, like most of the characters in the narrative from first to last, has been unable to sleep. And at the near corner of the house close to a never before remarked ventilator, is a hastily and inaccurately refilled excavation. . . .

"Then events come hurrying in a sort of tangled haste—making sibyl-like gestures.

"At the doorway Mutimer appears—swaying with some profound emotion. He is still in his evening attire. He has not yet gone to bed. In spite of the dawn he carries a burning candle—obliquely. At the sight of his master he withdraws—backwards and with difficulty. . . .

"Then," said Boon, "I get my crowning chapter: the breakfast, a peculiar *something,* something almost palpable in the atmosphere

—Deshman hoarse and a little talkative, Mimbleton with a possibly nervous headache, husky also and demanding tea in a thick voice, Mutimer waiting uneasily, and Mr. Blandish, outwardly calm, yet noting every particular, thinking meanings into every word and movement, and growing more and more clear in his conviction that *Mutimer knows—knows everything.* . . .

Mutimer as the plot thickens.

"Book two opens with Mr. Blandish practically in possession of the facts. Putting the thing coarsely, the treasure is—1813 brandy, in considerable quantities bricked up in a disused cellar of Samphire House. Samphire House, instead of being the fine claret of a refuge Mr. Blandish supposed, is a loaded port. But of course in the novel we shall not put things coarsely, and for a long time you will be by no means clear what the 'spirit' is that Mr. Blandish is now resolved to exorcise. He is, in fact, engaged in trying to get that brandy away, trying to de-alcoholize his existence, trying—if one must put the thing in all the concrete crudity of his fundamental intention—to sell the stuff. . . .

"Now in real life you would just go and sell it. But people in the novels of Henry James do not do things in the inattentive, offhand, rather confused, and partial way of reality: they bring enormous brains to bear upon the minutest particulars of existence. Mr. Blandish, following the laws of that world, has not simply to sell his brandy: he has to sell it subtly, intricately, interminably, with a delicacy, with a dignity. . . .

OF ART AND LITERATURE

"He consults friends—impalpable, intricate, inexhaustible friends.

"There are misunderstandings. One old and trusted intimate concludes rather hastily that Mr. Blandish is confessing that he has written a poem, another that he is making a proposal of marriage, another that he wishes an introduction to the secretary of the Psychical Research Society. . . . All this," said Boon, "remains, perhaps indefinitely, to be worked out. Only the end, the end, comes with a rush. Deshman has found for him— one never gets nearer to it than the 'real right people.' The real right people send their agent down, a curious blend of gentleman and commercial person he is, to investigate, to verify, to estimate quantities. Ultimately he will— shall we say it?—make an offer. With a sense of immense culmination the reader at last approaches the hoard. . . .

"You are never told the thing exactly. It is by indefinable suggestions, by exquisite approaches and startings back, by circumlocution the most delicate, that your mind at last shapes its realization, that—the last drop of the last barrel has gone and that Mutimer, the butler, lies dead or at least helpless—in the inner cellar. And a beautiful flavour, ripe and yet rare, rich without opulence, hangs—*diminuendo morendo*—in the air. . . . .

CHAPTER V

OF THE ASSEMBLING AND OPENING OF THE WORLD CONFERENCE ON THE MIND OF THE RACE

1

IT must be borne in mind that not even the opening chapter of this huge book, "The Mind of the Race," was ever completely written. The discussion in the Garden by the Sea existed merely so far as the fragment of dialogue I have quoted took it. I do not know what Mr. Gosse contributed except that it was something bright, and that presently he again lost his temper and washed his hands of the whole affair and went off with Mr. Yeats to do a little Academy thing of their own round a corner, and I do not know what became of the emissaries of Lord Northcliffe and Mr. Hearst. One conversation drops out of mind and another begins; it is like the battle of the Aisne passing slowly into the battle of the Yser. The idea develops into the holding of a definite congress upon the Mind of the Race at some central place. I don't think Boon was ever very clear whether that place was Chautauqua, or Grindelwald, or Stratford, or Oxford during the Long Vacation, or the Exhibition grounds at San Francisco. It was, at any rate, some such place, and it was a place that was speedily placarded with all sorts of bills and notices and counsels, such as, "To the Central Hall," or "Section B: Criticism and Reviewing," or "Section M: Prose Style," or "Authors' Society (British) Solicitors' Department," or "Exhibit of the Reading Room of the British Museum."

Manifestly the model of a meeting of the British Association for the Advancement of Science dominated his mind more and more, until at last he began to concoct a presidential address. And he invented a man called J. B. Pondlebury, very active and illiterate, but an excellent organizer, trained by Selfridge, that Marshall Field of London, who is very directive throughout. J. B. Pondlebury orders the special trains, contrives impossible excursions, organizes garden fêtes and water parties, keeps people together who would prefer to be separated, and breaks up people who have been getting together. Through all these things drifts Hallery, whose writings started the idea, and sometimes he is almost, as it were, leader and sometimes he is like a drowned body in the torrent below Niagara—Pondlebury being Niagara.

On the whole the atmosphere of the great conference was American, and yet I distinctly remember that it was the Special Train to Bâle of which he gave us an account one afternoon; it was a night journey of considerable eventfulness, with two adjacent carriages de luxe labelled respectively "Specially Reserved for Miss Marie Corelli," and "Specially Reserved for Mr. and Mrs. George Bernard Shaw," with conspicuous reiterations. The other compartments were less exclusive, and contained curious minglings of greatness, activity, and reputation. Sir J. M. Barrie had an upper berth in a *wagon-lit,* where he remained sympathetically silent above a crowd of younger reputations, a crowd too numerous to permit the making of the lower berth and overflowing into the corridor. I remember Boon kept jamming new people into that congestion. The whole train, indeed, was to be fearfully overcrowded. That was part of the joke. James Joyce I recall as a novelist strange to me that Boon insisted was a "first-rater." He represented him as being of immense size but extreme bashfulness. And he talked about D. H. Lawrence, St. John Ervine, Reginald Wright Kauffman, Leonard Merrick, Viola Meynell, Rose Macaulay, Katherine Mansfield, Mary Austin, Clutton Brock, Robert Lynd, James Stephens, Philip

Guedalla, H. M. Tomlinson, Denis Garstin, Dixon Scott, Rupert Brooke, Geoffrey Young, F. S. Flint, Marmaduke Pickthall, Randolph S. Bourne, James Milne——

"Through all the jam, I think we must have Ford Madox Hueffer, wandering to and fro up and down the corridor, with distraught blue eyes, laying his hands on heads and shoulders, the Only Uncle of the Gifted Young, talking in a languid, plangent tenor, now boasting about trivialities, and now making familiar criticisms (which are invariably ill-received), and occasionally quite absent-mindedly producing splendid poetry." . . .

Like most authors who have made their way to prominence and profit, Boon was keenly sympathetic with any new writer who promised to do interesting work, and very ready with his praise and recognition. That disposition in these writing, prolific times would alone have choked the corridor. And he liked young people even when their promises were not exactly convincing. He hated to see a good book neglected, and was for ever ramming "The Crystal Age" and "Said the Fisherman" and "Tony Drum" and "George's Mother" and "A Hind Let Loose" and "Growing Pains" down the throats of his visitors. But there were very human and definite limits to his appreciations. Conspicuous success, and particularly conspicuous respectable success, chilled his generosity. Conrad he could not endure. I do him no wrong in mentioning that; it is the way with most of us; and a score of flourishing contemporaries who might have liked tickets for the Conference special would have found great difficulty in getting them.

There is a fascination in passing judgments and drawing up class lists. For a time the high intention of the Mind of the Race was forgotten while we talked the narrow "shop" of London literary journalism, and discovered and weighed and log-rolled and—in the case of the more established—blamed and condemned. That Bâle train became less and less like a train and more and more like a descriptive catalogue.

For the best part of an afternoon we talked of the young and the new, and then we fell into a discussion about such reputations as Pickthall's and W. H. Hudson's and the late Stephen Crane's, reputations ridiculously less than they ought to be, so that these writers, who are certainly as securely classic as Beckford or Herrick, are still unknown to half the educated English reading public. Was it due to the haste of criticism or the illiteracy of publishers? That question led us so far away from the special Bâle train that we never returned to it. But I know that we decided that the real and significant writers were to be only a small portion of the crowd that congested the train; there were also to be endless impostors, imitators, editors, raiders of the world of print. . . . At every important station there was to be a frightful row about all these people's tickets, and violent attempts to remove doubtful cases. . . . Then Mr. Clement K. Shorter was to come in to advise and help the conductor. . . . Ultimately this led to trouble about Mr. Shorter's own credentials. . . .

Some of Boon's jokes about this train were, to say the best of them, obvious. Mr. Compton Mackenzie was in trouble about his excess luggage, for example. Mr. Upton Sinclair, having carried out his ideal of an innocent frankness to a logical completeness in his travelling equipment, was forcibly wrapped in blankets by the train officials. Mr. Thomas Hardy had a first-class ticket but travelled by choice or mistake in a second-class compartment, his deserted place being subsequently occupied by that promising young novelist Mr. Hugh Walpole, provided with a beautiful fur rug, a fitted dressing-bag, a writing slope, a gold-nibbed fountain pen, innumerable introductions, and everything that a promising young novelist can need. The brothers Chesterton, Mr. Maurice Baring, and Mr. Belloc sat up all night in the *wagon-restaurant* con-

suming beer enormously and conversing upon
immortality and whether it extends to Semitic
and Oriental persons. At the end of the train,
I remember, there was to have been a horse-
van containing Mr. Maurice Hewlett's charger
—Mr. Hewlett himself, I believe, was left behind by accident at the Gare de Lyons—Mr.
Cunninghame Graham's Arab steed, and a
large, quiet sheep, the inseparable pet of Mr.
Arthur Christopher Benson. . . .

There was also, I remember, a description
of the whole party running for early coffee,
which gave Boon ample and regrettable op-
portunities for speculations upon the *désha-
bille* of his contemporaries. Much of the detail of that invention I prefer to forget, but I
remember Mr. Shaw was fully prepared for
the emerging with hand-painted pyjamas, over
which he was wearing a saffron dressing-gown
decorated in green and purple scrolls by one
of the bolder artists associated with Mr. Roger
Fry, and as these special train allusions are all
that I can ever remember Boon saying about

Shaw, and as the drawing does in itself amount to a criticism, I give it here. . . .

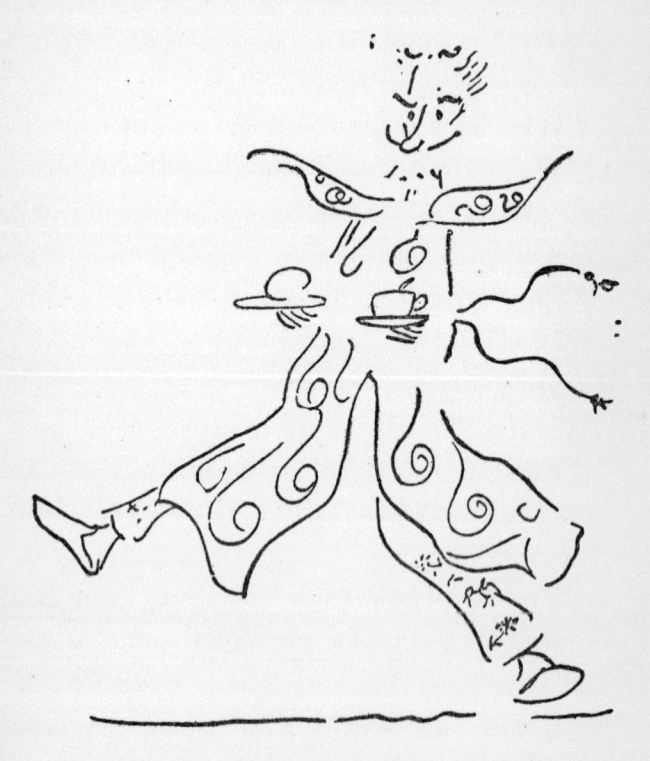

How Mr. Shaw knocked them all on Bâle platform, and got right into the middle of the picture. Remark his earnest face. This surely is no mountebank.

2

BOON was greatly exercised over the problem of a president.

"Why have a president?" Dodd helped.

"There must be a Presidential Address," said Boon, "and these things always do have a president."

"Lord Rosebery," suggested Wilkins.

"Lord Morley," said Dodd.

"Lord Bryce."

Then we looked at one another.

"For my own part," said Boon, "if we are going in for that sort of thing, I favour Lord Reay.

"You see, Lord Reay has never done anything at all connected with literature. Morley and Bryce and Rosebery have at any rate written things—historical studies, addresses, things like that—but Reay has never written anything, and he let Gollancz make him president of the British Academy without a murmur.

[141]

This seems to mark him out for this further distinction. He is just the sort of man who would be made—and who would let himself be made—president of a British affair of this sort, and they would hoist him up and he would talk for two or three hours without a blush. Just like that other confounded peer—what was his name?—who bored and bored and bored at the Anatole France dinner. . . . In the natural course of things it would be one of these literary lords. . . ."

"What would he say?" asked Dodd.

"Maunderings, of course. It will make the book rather dull. I doubt if I can report him at length. . . . He will speak upon contemporary letters, the lack of current achievement. . . . I doubt if a man like Lord Reay ever reads at all. One wonders sometimes what these British literary aristocrats do with all their time. Probably he left off reading somewhere in the eighties. He won't have noted it, of course, and he will be under the impression that nothing has been written for the past thirty years."

"Good Lord!" said Wilkins.

"And he'll say that. Slowly. Steadily. Endlessly. Then he will thank God for the English classics, ask where now is our Thackeray? where now our Burns? our Charlotte Brontë? our Tennyson? say a good word for our immortal bard, and sit down amidst the loud applause of thousands of speechlessly furious British and American writers. . . ."

"I don't see that this will help your book forward," said Dodd.

"No, but it's a proper way of beginning. Like Family Prayers."

"I suppose," said Wilkins, "if you told a man of that sort that there were more and better poets writing in English beautifully in 1914 than ever before he wouldn't believe it. I suppose if you said that Ford Madox Hueffer, for example, had produced sweeter and deeper poetry than Alfred, Lord Tennyson, he'd have a fit."

"He'd have nothing of the kind. You could no more get such an idea into the head of one of these great vestiges of our Gladstonian days than you could get it into the seat of a Windsor chair. . . . And people don't have fits unless something has got into them. . . . No, he'd reflect quite calmly that first of all he'd never heard of this Hueffer, then that probably he was a very young man. And, anyhow, one didn't meet him in important places. . . . And after inquiry he would find out he was a journalist. . . . And then probably he'd cease to cerebrate upon the question. . . ."

3

"BESIDES," said Boon, "we must have one of our literary peers because of America."

"You're unjust to America," I said.

"No," said Boon. "But Aunt Dove—I know her ways."

That led to a long, rambling discussion about the American literary atmosphere. Nothing that I could say would make him relent from his emphatic assertion that it is a spinster atmosphere, an atmosphere in which you can't say all sorts of things and where all sorts of things have to be specially phrased. "And she can't stand young things and crude things——"

"America!" said Wilkins.

"The America I mean. The sort of America that ought to supply young new writers with caresses and—nourishment. . . . Instead of which you get the *Nation*. . . .

That bleak acidity, that refined appeal to take the child away."

"But they don't produce new young writers!" said Wilkins.

"But they do!" said Boon. "And they strangle them!"

It was extraordinary what a power metaphors and fancies had upon Boon. Only those who knew him intimately can understand how necessary Miss Bathwick was to him. He would touch a metaphor and then return and sip it, and then sip and drink and swill until it had intoxicated him hopelessly.

"America," said Boon, "can produce such a supreme writer as Stephen Crane—the best writer of English for the last half-century— or Mary Austin, who used to write—What other woman could touch her? But America won't own such children. It's amazing. It's a case of concealment of birth. She exposes them. Whether it's Shame—or a Chinese trick. . . . She'll sit never knowing she's had a Stephen Crane, adoring the European reputation, the florid mental gestures of a Conrad. You see, she can tell Conrad 'writes.' It shows. And she'll let Mary Austin die of neglect, while she worships the 'art' of Mary Ward. It's like turning from the feet of a goddess to a pair of goloshes. She firmly believes that old quack Bergson is a bigger man than her own unapproachable William James. . . . She's incredible. I tell you it's only conceivable on one supposition. . . . I'd never thought before about these disgraceful sidelights on Miss Dove's career. . . .

"We English do make foundlings of some of her little victims, anyhow. . . . But why hasn't she any natural instinct in the matter?

"Now, if one represented that peculiar Bostonian intellectual gentility, the *Nation* kind of thing, as a very wicked, sour lady's-maid with a tremendous influence over the Spinster's conduct. . . ."

His mind was running on.

"I begin to see a melodramatic strain in this great novel, *Miss Dove*. . . . *Miss Dove's*

Derelicts. . . . Too broad, I am afraid. If one were to represent Sargent and Henry James as two children left out one cold night in a basket at a cottage in the village by a mysterious stranger, with nothing but a roll of dollars and a rough drawing of the Washington coat-of-arms to indicate their parentage. . . .

"Then when they grow up they go back to the big house and she's almost kind to them. . . .

"Have you ever read the critical articles of Edgar Allan Poe? They're very remarkable. He is always demanding an American Literature. It is like a deserted baby left to die in its cradle, weeping and wailing for its bottle. . . . What he wanted, of course, was honest and intelligent criticism.

"To this day America kills her Poes. . . ."

"But confound it!" said Wilkins, "America does make discoveries for herself. Hasn't she discovered Lowes Dickinson?"

"But that merely helps my case. Lowes Dickinson has just the qualities that take the

American judgment; he carries the shadow of King's College Chapel about with him wherever he goes; he has an unobtrusive air of being doubly starred in Baedeker and not thinking anything of it. And also she took Noyes to her bosom. But when has American criticism ever had the intellectual pluck to proclaim an American?

"And so, you see," he remarked, going off again at a tangent, "if we are going to bid for American adhesions there's only one course open to us in the matter of this presidential address . . . Lord Morley." . . .

"You're a little difficult to follow at times," said Wilkins.

"Because he's the man who's safest not to say anything about babies or—anything alive. . . . Obviously a literary congress in America must be a festival in honour of sterility.

"Aunt Dove demands it. Like celebrating the virginity of Queen Elizabeth." . . .

4

I FIND among the fragments of my departed friend some notes that seem to me to be more or less relevant here. They are an incomplete report of the proceedings of a section S, devoted to *Poiometry,* apparently the scientific measurement of literary greatness. It seems to have been under the control of a special committee, including Mr. James Huneker, Mr. Slosson, Sir Thomas Seccombe, Mr. James Douglas, Mr. Clement K. Shorter, the acting editor of the *Bookman,* and the competition editress of the *Westminster Gazette.* . . .

Apparently the notes refer to some paper read before the section. Its authorship is not stated, nor is there any account of its reception. But the title is "The Natural History of Greatness, with especial reference to Literary Reputations."

The opening was evidently one of those

rapid historical sketches frequent in such papers.

"Persuasion that human beings are sometimes of disproportionate size appears first in the Egyptian and Syrian wall paintings. . . . Probably innate. . . . The discouragement of the young a social necessity in all early societies. In all societies? . . . Exaggerated stories about the departed. . . . Golden ages. Heroic ages. Ancestor worship. . . . Dead dogs better than living lions. . . . Abraham. Moses. The Homeric reputation, the first great literary cant. Resentment against Homer's exaggerated claims on the part of intelligent people. Zoilus. Caricature of the Homerists in the Satyricon. Other instances of unorthodox ancient criticism. . . . Shakespeare as an intellectual nuisance. . . . Extreme suffering caused to contemporary writers by the Shakespeare legend. . . .

"Another form of opposition to these obsessions is the creation of countervailing reputations. Certain people in certain ages have resolved to set up Great Men of their own to put beside these Brocken spectres from the past. This marks a certain stage of social development, the beginning of self-consciousness in a civilized community. Self-criticism always begins in self-flattery. Virgil as an early instance of a Great Man of set intentions; deliberately put up as the Latin Homer. . . .

"Evolution of the greatness of Aristotle during the Middle Ages.

"Little sense of contemporary Greatness among the Elizabethans.

"Comparison with the past the prelude to Great-Man-Making, begins with such a work as Swift's 'Battle of the Books.' Concurrently the decline in religious feeling robs the past of its half-mystical prestige. The Western world ripe for Great Men in the early nineteenth century. The Germans as a highly competitive and envious people take the lead. The inflation of Schiller. The greatness of Goethe. Incredible dullness of 'Elective Affinities,' of 'Werther,' of 'Wilhelm Meister's Apprenticeship.' The second part of 'Faust' a tiresome muddle. Large pretentiousness of the man's career. Resolve of the Germans to have a Great Fleet, a Great Empire, a Great Man. Difficulty in finding a suitable German for Greatening. Expansion of the Goethe legend. German efficiency brought to bear on the task. Lectures. Professors. Goethe compared to Shakespeare. Compared to Homer. Compared to Christ. Compared to God. Discovered to be incomparable. . . .

"Stimulation of Scotch activities. The Scotch also passionately and aggressively patriotic. Fortunate smallness of Scotland and lack of adjacent docile Germans has alone saved the world from another Prussia. Desperation of the search for a real Scotch First Rater. The discovery that Burns was as great as Shakespeare. Greater. The booming of Sir Walter Scott. Wake up, England! The production of Dickens. The slow but enormous discovery of Wordsworth. Victorian age sets up as a rival to the Augustine. Selection of Great Men in every department. The Great Victorian painters. Sir Frederick Leighton, compared with Titian and Michael Angelo. Tennyson as Virgil. Lord Tennyson at the crest of the Victorian Greatness wave. His hair. His cloak. His noble bearing. His aloofness. His Great Pipe. His price per word. His intellectual familiarities with Queen Victoria. . . .

"Longfellow essentially an American repartee. . . .

"Ingratitude of British Royal Family to those who contributed to the Victorian Greatness period, shown in the absence of representative Great Men from the Buckingham Palace Monument. Victoria did not do it all. Compare the Albert Memorial. . . .

"Interesting task to plan an alternative pedestal. Proposal to make designs for a monument to our own times. Symbolic corner groups by Will Dyson. Frieze of representative men by Max. Canopy by Wyndham

Lewis. Lost opportunity for much bright discussion. . . .

"Analysis of literary greatness. Is any literary achievement essential to greatness? Probably a minute minimum indispensable. Burns. Fitzgerald. But compare Lord Acton and Lord Reay. Necessity of a marked personality. Weaknesses, but no unpopular vices. Greatness blighted by want of dignity. Laurence Sterne. Reciprocal duty of those made Great not to distress their Public. But imperfectly established scandal or complexity of relationship may give scope for vindications and research. Or a certain irregularity of life may create a loyal and devoted following of sympathizers. Shelley. . . . Then capable advocacy is needed and a critical world large enough to be effective but small enough to be unanimous. Part an able publisher may play in establishing and developing a Great Man. . . . Quiet Push, not Noisy Push. Injury done by tactless advertisement. . . . The element of luck. . . .

"These are the seeds of greatness, but the growth depends upon the soul. The best soil is a large uncritical public newly come to reading, a little suspicious of the propriety of the practice and in a state of intellectual snobbishness. It must also be fairly uniform and on some common basis of ideas. Ideally represented by the reading publics of Germany, Britain, the United States, and France in the middle nineteenth century. . . .

"Decline in the output of Greatness towards the end of the Victorian time. Probably due in all cases to an enlargement of the reading public to unmanageable dimensions. No reputation sufficiently elastic to cover it. The growth of Chicago, New York, and the West destroyed the preponderance of Boston in America, and the Civil War broke the succession of American Great Men. Rarity of new American-born Greatnesses after the war. Dumping of established greatnesses from England gave no chance to the native market. No Protection for America in this respect. In

THE WORLD CONFERENCE

Great Britain the board schools create big masses of intelligent people inaccessible to the existing machinery by which Greatness is imposed. The Greatness output in Britain declines also in consequence. Mrs. Humphry Ward, the last of the British Victorian Great. Expressed admiration of Mr. Gladstone for her work. Support of the *Spectator*. Profound respect of the American people. Rumour that she is represented as a sea goddess at the base of the Queen Victoria Memorial unfounded. Nobody is represented on the Queen Victoria Memorial except Queen Victoria. . . . Necessity after the epoch of Mrs. Ward of more and more flagrant advertisement to reach the enlarged public, so that at last touch is lost with the critical centres. Great Men beyond the Limit. Self-exploded candidates for Greatness. Boomsters. Best Sellers. Mr. Hall Caine as the shocking example. . . .

"Other causes contributing to the decay of Greatness among literary men. Competition of politicians, princes, personages generally for the prestige of the literary man. Superior initial advantage in conspicuousness. The genuine writer handicapped. The process already beginning at the crest of the period. Queen Victoria's 'Leaves from a Highland Diary.' Mr. Gladstone and the higher windiness. Later developments. The Kaiser as a man of letters. Mr. Roosevelt as writer and critic. The Essays of President Wilson. The case of Lord Rosebery. Mr. Haldane as a philosopher. As a critic. His opinion of Goethe. Compare the royal and noble authors of Byzantium. Compare the Roman Emperor becoming Pontifex Maximus. Compare the cannibal chief in a general's hat. . . .

"Return of the literary men as such to a decent obscurity. From which they are unlikely to emerge again. This an unmixed blessing. So long as good writing and sound thinking are still appreciated the less we hear about authors the better. Never so little recognized Greatness and never so much wise, subtle, sweet, and boldly conceived literary work as now. This will probably continue. [He was writing before the war.] The English-reading literary world too large now for the operations of Greatening. Doubtful case of Rabindranath Tagore. Discuss this. Special suitability of India as a basis for Greatness. India probably on the verge of a Greatness period. . . .

"Disrespect a natural disposition in the young. Checked and subdued in small societies, but now happily rampant in the uncontrollable English-speaking communities. The new (undignified) criticism. The *English Review*. Mr. Austin Harrison and the street-boy style. The literature of the chalked fence. The *New Age*. Literary carbolic acid—with an occasional substitution of vitriol. . . . Insurrection of the feminine mind against worship. Miss Rebecca West as the last birth of time. A virile-minded generation of young women indicated. Mrs. Humphry Ward blushes publicly for the *Freewoman* in the

Times. Hitherto Greatness has demanded the applause of youth and feminine worship as necessary conditions. As necessary to its early stages as down to an eider chick. Impossible to imagine Incipient Greatness nestling comfortably upon Orage, Austin Harrison, and Rebecca West. Dearth of young Sidney Colvins. . . . Unhappy position of various derelict and still imperfectly developed Great surviving from the old times. Arnold Bennett as an aborted Great Man. Would have made a Great Victorian and had a crowd of satellite helpers. Now no one will ever treasure his old hats and pipes. . . .

"Idea of an experimental resurrection of those who still live in our hearts. If Goethe had a second time on earth——? Could he do it now? Would Lord Haldane perceive him? Imaginary description of Lord Haldane's recognition of a youthful Goethe. They meet by accident during a walking tour in Germany. Amiable aloofness of Lord Haldane. His gradual discovery of an intellectual superior in his modest companion. Public proclamation of his find. . . . Doubts. . . .

"Peroration. Will the world be happy without Literary Greatnesses? Improvise and take a cheerful line upon this question."

Miss Rebecca West, pensive, after writing her well-known opinion of that Great Good Woman-Soul, Miss Ellen Key.

5

ULTIMATELY, against every possibility of the case, Boon decided that the President of his conference must be Hallery. And he wrote his presidential address. But he never read that address to us. Some shyness I think restrained him. I dig it out here now for the first time, a little astonished at it, disposed to admire something in its spirit. . . . But yet one has to admit that it shows an extraordinary lapse from Boon's accustomed mocking humour.

Here is the opening.

"Hallery then advanced to the edge of the platform and fumbled with his manuscript. His face was very white and his expression bitterly earnest. With an appearance of effort he began, omitting in his nervousness any form of address to his audience—

" 'For the most part, the life of human communities has been as unconscious as the life of animals. They have been born as unknowingly as the beasts; they have followed unforeseen and unheeded destinies, and destruction has come to them from forces scarcely anticipated and not understood. Tribes, nations beyond counting, have come and passed, with scarcely a mental activity beyond a few legends, a priestly guess at cosmogony, a few rumours and traditions, a list of kings as bare as a schoolboy's diary, a war or so, a triumph or so. . . . We are still only in the beginning of history—in the development, that is, of a racial memory; we have as yet hardly begun to inquire into our racial origins, our racial conditions, our racial future. . . . Philosophy, which is the discussion of the relation of the general to the particular, of the whole to the part, of the great and yet vague life of the race to the intense yet manifestly incomplete life of the individual, is still not three thousand years old. Man has lived consciously as man it may be for hundreds of thousands of years, he has learnt of himself by talking to his fellows, he has expressed personal love and many personal feelings with a truth and beauty that are well nigh final, but the race does but begin to live as a conscious being. It begins to live as a conscious being, and as it does so, the individual too begins to live in a new way, a greater, more understanding, and more satisfying way. His thoughts apprehend interests beyond himself and beyond his particular life.' . . .

"At this point Hallery became so acutely aware of his audience that for some seconds he could not go on reading. A number of people in various parts of the hall had suddenly given way to their coughs, a bald-headed gentleman about the middle of the assembly had discovered a draught, and was silently but conspicuously negotiating for the closing of a window by an attendant, and at the back a cultivated-looking young gentleman was stealing out on tiptoe.

The first departure.

"For a moment Hallery was distressed by the thought that perhaps he might have taken a more amusing line than the one he had chosen, and then, realizing how vain were such regrets and rather quickening his pace, he resumed the reading of his address—

"'You see that I am beginning upon a very comprehensive scale, for I propose to bring within the scope of this conference all that arises out of these two things, out of the realization of the incompleteness of man's individual life on the one hand and out of the realization of a greater being in which man lives, of a larger racial life and ampler references upon the other. All this much—and with a full awareness of just how much it is—I am going to claim as literature and our province. Religion, I hold, every religion so far as it establishes and carries ideas, is literature, philosophy is literature, science is literature; a pamphlet or a leading article. I put all these things together——'

"At this point there was a second departure.

The second departure.

Almost immediately followed by a third.

The third departure.

"Hallery halted for a second time and then gripped the reading-desk with both hands, and, reading now with a steadily accelerated velocity, heeded his audience no more—

"'I put all these things together because, indeed, it is only associations of antiquity and prescription and prestige can separate them. Altogether they constitute the great vague body of man's super-personal mental life, his

unselfish life, his growing life, as a premeditating, self-conscious race and destiny. Here in growing volume, in this comprehensive literature of ours, preserved, selected, criticized, restated, continually rather more fined, continually rather more clarified, we have the mind, not of a mortal but of an immortal adventurer. Whom for the moment, fractionally, infinitesimally, whenever we can forget ourselves in pure feeling, in service, in creative effort or disinterested thought, we are privileged in that measure to become. This wonder that we celebrate, this literature, is the dawn of human divinity. . . . .
. . . . , "

But though Hallery went on, I do not, on reflection, think that I will. I doubt if Boon ever decided to incorporate this extraordinary Presidential Address in our book; I think perhaps he meant to revise it or substitute something else. He wanted to state a case for the extreme importance of literature, and to my mind he carried his statement into regions mystical, to say the least of it, and likely to be considered blasphemous by many quite right-minded people. For instance, he made Hallery speak of the Word that links men's minds. He brings our poor, mortal, mental activities into the most extraordinary relationship with those greater things outside our lives which it is our duty to revere as much as possible and to think about as little as possible; he draws no line between them. . . . He never, I say, read the paper to us. . . . I cannot guess whether he did not read it to us because he doubted himself or because he doubted us, and I do not even care to examine my own mind to know whether I do or do not believe in the thesis he sets so unhesitatingly down. In a sense it is no doubt true that literature is a kind of overmind of the race, and in a sense, no doubt, the Bible and the Koran, the Talmud and the Prayer Book are literature. In a sense Mr. Upton Sinclair's "Bible" for Socialists of bits from ancient and modern writings is literature. In a sense, too, literature does go on rather like a continuous mind thinking. . . . But I feel that all this is just in a sense. . . . I don't really believe it. I am not quite sure what I do really believe, but I certainly recoil from anything so crudely positive as Hallery's wild assertions. . . . It would mean worshipping literature. Or at least worshipping the truth in literature. . . .

Of course, one knows that real literature is something that has to do with leisure and cultivated people and books and shaded lamps and all that sort of thing. But Hallery wants to drag in not only cathedrals and sanctuaries, but sky-signs and hoardings. . . . He wants literature to embrace whatever is in or whatever changes the mind of the race, except purely personal particulars. And I think Boon was going to make Hallery claim this, just in order to show up against these tremendous significances the pettiness of the contemporary literary life, the poverty and levity of criticism, the mean business side of modern book-making and book-selling. . . .

Turning over the pages of this rejected address, which I am sure the reader would not thank me for printing, I do come upon this presentable passage, which illustrates what I am saying—

"So that every man who writes to express or change or criticize an idea, every man who observes and records a fact in the making of a research, every man who hazards or tests a theory, every artist of any sort who really expresses, does thereby, in that very act, participate, share in, become for just that instant when he is novel and authentically *true,* the Mind of the Race, the thinking divinity. Do you not see, then, what an arrogant worship, what a sacramental thing it is to lift up brain and hand and say, '*I too will add*'? We bring our little thoughts as the priest brings a piece of common bread to consecration, and though we have produced but a couplet or a dozen lines of prose, we have nevertheless done the parallel miracle. And all reading that is reading with the mind, all conscious subjugation of our attention to expressed beauty, or expressed truth, is sacramental, is communion with the immortal being. We lift up our thoughts out of the little festering pit of desire and vanity which is one's individual self into that greater self." . . .

So he talks, and again presently of "that world-wide immortal communion incessant as the march of sun and planets amidst the stars." . . .

And then, going on with his vast comparison, for I cannot believe this is more than a fantastic parallelism: "And if the mind that does, as we say, create is like the wafer that has become miraculously divine, then though you may not like to think of it, all you who give out books, who print books and collect books, and sell books and lend them, who bring pictures to people's eyes, set things forth in theatres, hand out thought in any way from the thinking to the attentive mind, all you are priests, you do a priestly office, and every bookstall and hoarding is a wayside shrine, offering consolation and release to men and women from the intolerable prison of their narrow selves." . . .

6

THAT, I think, is what Boon really at the bottom of his heart felt and believed about literature.

And yet in some way he could also not believe it; he could recognize something about it that made him fill the margin of the manuscript of this address with grotesque figures of an imaginary audience going out. They were, I know, as necessary to his whole conception as his swinging reference to the stars; both were as much part of his profound belief as the gargoyle on the spire and the high altar are necessary parts of a Gothic cathedral. And among other figures I am amused rather than hurt to find near the end this of myself—

Too high-pitched even for Reginald.

CHAPTER VI

OF NOT LIKING HALLERY AND THE ROYAL SOCIETY FOR THE DISCOURAGEMENT OF LITERATURE

1

IN the same peculiar receptacle in which I find this presidential address I found a quantity of other papers and scraps of paper, upon which Boon, I should judge, had been thinking about that address and why he was ashamed to produce it to us, and why he perceived that this audience would dislike Hallery so much that he was obliged to admit that they would go out before his lecture was finished, and why he himself didn't somehow like this Hallery that he had made. All these

[177]

writings are in the nature of fragments, some are illegible and more are incomprehensible; but it is clear that his mind attacked these questions with a most extraordinary width of reference. I find him writing about the One and the Many, the General and the Particular, the Species and the Individual, declaring that it is through "the dimensions (*sic*) of space and time" that "individuation" becomes possible, and citing Darwin, Heraclitus, Kant, Plato, and Tagore, all with a view to determining just exactly what it was that irritated people in the breadth and height and expression of Hallery's views. Or to be more exact, what he knew would have irritated people with these views if they had ever been expressed.

Here is the sort of thing that I invite the intelligent reader to link up if he can with the very natural phenomenon of a number of quite ordinary sensible people hostile and in retreat before a tedious, perplexing, and presumptuous discourse—

"The individual human mind spends itself about equally in headlong flight from the Universal, which it dreads as something that will envelop and subjugate it, and in headlong flight to the Universal, which it seeks as a refuge from its own loneliness and silliness. It knows very certainly that the Universal will ultimately comprehend and incorporate it, yet it desires always that the Universal should *mother* it, take it up without injuring it in the slightest degree, foment and nourish its egotism, cherish fondly all its distinctions, give it all the kingdoms of existence to play with. . . .

"Ordinary people snuggle up to God as a lost leveret in a freezing wilderness might snuggle up to a Siberian tiger. . . .

"You see that man who flies and seeks, who needs and does not want, does at last get to a kind of subconscious compromise over the matter. Couldn't he perhaps get the Infinite with the chill off? Couldn't he perhaps find a warm stuffed tiger? He cheats himself by hiding in what he can pretend is the goal. So he tries to escape from the pursuit of the living God to dead gods, evades religion in a church, does his best to insist upon time-honoured formulæ; God must have a button on the point. And it is our instinctive protection of the subconscious arrangement that makes us so passionately resentful at raw religion, at crude spiritual realities, at people who come at us saying harsh understandable things about these awful matters. . . . *They may wake the tiger!* . . .

We like to think of religion as something safely specialized, codified, and put away. Then we can learn the rules and kick about a bit. But when some one comes along saying that science is religion, literature is religion, business—they'll come to that presently!—business is religion! . . .

"It spoils the afternoon. . . .

"But that alone does not explain why Hallery, delivering his insistent presidential address, is detestable to his audience—for it is quite clear that he is detestable. I'm certain of it. No, what is the matter there is that the aggression of the universal is pointed and embittered by an all too justifiable suspicion that the individual who maintains it is still more aggressive, has but armed himself with the universal in order to achieve our discomfiture. . . . It's no good his being modest; that only embitters it. It is no good his making disavowals; that only shows that he is aware of it. . . .

"Of course I invented Hallery only to get this burthen off myself. . . .

"All spiritual truths ought to be conveyed by a voice speaking out of a dark void. As Hardy wants his spirits to speak in the *Dynasts*. Failing that, why should we not deal with these questions through the anonymity of a gramophone? . . .

"A modern religion founded on a mysterious gramophone which was discovered carefully packed in a box of peculiar construction on a seat upon Primrose Hill. . . .

"How well the great organized religions have understood this! How sound is the effort to meet it by shaving a priest's head or obliging him to grow a beard, putting him into canonicals, drilling him and regimenting him, so as to make him into a mere type. . . .

"If I were to found a religion, I think I should insist upon masked priests." . . .

2

THIS idea that the defensive instinct of the individuality, Jealousy, is constantly at war not only with other individualities but with all the great de-individualizing things, with Faith, with Science, with Truth, with Beauty; that out of its resentments and intricate devices one may draw the explanation of most of the perplexities and humours of the intellectual life, indeed the explanation of most life and of most motives, is the quintessence of Boon. The Mind of the Race toils through this jungle of jealous individuality to emerge. And the individual, knowing that single-handed he hasn't a chance against the immortal, allies himself with this and that, with sham immortalities, and partially effaced and partially confuted general things. And so it sets up its Greatnesses, to save it from greatness, its solemnities to preserve it from the overwhelming gravity of truth. "See," it can say, "I have my gods already, thank you. I do not think we will discuss this matter further."

I admit the difficulty of following Boon in this. I admit, too, that I am puzzled about his Mind of the Race. Does he mean by that expression a Great Wisdom and Will that must be, or a Great Wisdom and Will that might be?

But here he goes on with the topic of Hallery again.

"I invented Hallery to get rid of myself, but, after all, Hallery is really no more than the shadow of myself, and if I were impersonal and well bred, and if I spoke behind a black screen, it would still be as much my voice as ever. I do not see how it is possible to prevent the impersonal things coming by and through persons; but at any rate we can begin to recognize that the person who brings the message is only in his way like the messenger boy who brings the telegrams. The writer may have a sensitive mind, the messenger boy may have nimble heels; that does not make him the creator of the thing that comes. Then I think people will be able to listen to such lectures as this of Hallery's without remembering all the time that it's a particular human being with a white face and a lisp. . . . And perhaps they will be able to respect literature and fine thought for the sake of the general human mind for which they live and for the sake of their own receptiveness." . . .

3

AND from that Boon suddenly went off into absurdities.

"Should all literature be anonymous?" he asks at the head of a sheet of notes.

"But one wants an author's name as a brand. Perhaps a number would suffice. Would authors write if they remained unknown? Mixed motives. Could one run a church with an unsalaried priesthood? But certainly now the rewards are too irregular, successful authors are absurdly flattered and provoked to impossible ambitions. Could we imitate the modern constitutional State by permitting limited ambitions but retaining all the higher positions inaccessible to mere enterprise and merit? Hereditary Novelists, Poets, and Philosophers, for example. The real ones undistinguished. Hereditary Historians and Scientific Men are already practical reality. Then such mischievous rewards and singlings out as the Nobel Prize could be distributed among these Official Intellectuals by lot or (better) by seniority. It would prevent much heart-burning." . . .

These last notes strike me as an extraordinary declension from the, at least, exalted argument of the preceding memoranda. But they do serve to emphasize the essence of—what shall I call it?—Boonism, the idea that there is a great collective mental process going on in many minds, and that it is impertinent and distracting to single out persons, great men, groups and schools, coteries and Academies. The flame burns wide and free. It is here; it is gone. You had it; you have it not. And again you see it plainly, stretching wide across the horizon. . . .

4

BUT after these scrappy notes about Jealousy and how people protect their minds against ideas, and especially the idea which is God, and against the mental intrusions of their fellow-creatures conveying ideas, I understand better the purport of that uninvited society, which he declared insisted upon coming to the Great Conference upon the Mind of the Race, and which held such enthusiastic and crowded meetings that at last it swamped all the rest of the enterprise. It was, he declared, to the bitter offence of Dodd, a society with very much the same attitude towards all impersonal mental activities that the Rationalist Press Association has to Religion, and it was called the Royal Society for the Discouragement of Literature.

"Why 'Royal'?" I asked.

"Oh—obviously," he said. . . .

This Royal Society was essentially an organization of the conservative instincts of man. Its aim was to stop all this thinking. . . .

And yet in some extraordinary way that either I did not note at the time or that he never explained, it became presently the whole Conference! The various handbills, pamphlets in outline, notes for lectures, and so forth, that accompanied his notes of the Proceedings of the Royal Society may either be intended as part of the sectional proceedings of the great conference or as the production of this hostile organization. I will make a few extracts from the more legible of these memoranda which render the point clearer.

5

PUBLISHERS AND BOOK DISTRIBUTORS

(Comparable to the Priest who hands the Elements and as much upon their Honour.)

THE Publisher regrets that the copy for this section is missing, and fears that the substance of it must be left to the imagination of the reader. This is the more regrettable as the section was probably of a highly technical nature.

6

THE YOUNG REVIEWER

HERE, again, Mr. Boon's notes are not to be found, and repeated applications to Mr. Bliss have produced nothing but a vague telegram to "go ahead."

7
THE SCHOOLMASTER AND LITERATURE

ESSENTIALLY the work of the schoolmaster is to prepare the young and naturally overindividualized mind for communion with the Mind of the Race. Essentially his curriculum deals with modes of expression, with languages, grammar, the mathematical system of statement, the various scientific systems of statement, the common legend of history. All leads up, as the scholar approaches adolescence, to the introduction to living literature, living thought, criticism, and religion. But when we consider how literature is taught in schools——"

Here the writing leaves off abruptly, and then there is written in very minute letters far down the page and apparently after an interval for reflection—

"Scholastic humour

O God!"

CHAPTER VII

WILKINS MAKES CERTAIN OBJECTIONS

1

WILKINS the author began to think about the Mind of the Race quite suddenly. He made an attack upon Boon as we sat in the rose-arbour smoking after lunch. Wilkins is a man of a peculiar mental constitution; he alternates between a brooding sentimental egotism and a brutal realism, and he is as weak and false in the former mood as he is uncompromising in the latter. I think the attraction that certainly existed between him and Boon must have been the attraction of opposites, for Boon is as emotional and sentimental in relation to the impersonal aspects of life as he is pitiless in relation to himself. Wilkins still spends large portions of his time thinking solemnly about some ancient trouble in which he was treated unjustly; I believe I once knew what it was, but I have long since forgotten. Yet when his mind does get loose from his own "case" for a bit it is, I think, a very penetrating mind indeed. And, at any rate, he gave a lot of exercise to Boon.

"All through this book, Boon," he began.

"What book?" asked Dodd.

"This one we are in. All through this book you keep on at the idea of the Mind of the Race. It is what the book is about; it is its theme. Yet I don't see exactly what you are driving at. Sometimes you seem to be making out this Mind of the Race to be a kind of God——"

"A synthetic God," said Boon. "If it is to be called a God at all."

Dodd nodded as one whose worst suspicions are confirmed.

"Then one has to assume it is a continuing,

coherent mind, that is slowly becoming wider, saner, profounder, more powerful?"

Boon never liked to be pressed back upon exact statements. "Yes," he said reluctantly. "In general—on the whole—yes. What are you driving at?"

"It includes all methods of expression from the poster when a play is produced at His Majesty's Theatre, from the cheering of the crowd when a fireman rescues a baby, up to —Walter Pater."

"So far as Pater expresses anything," said Boon.

"Then you go on from the elevation this idea of a secular quasi-divine racial mental progress gives you, to judge and condemn all sorts of decent artistic and literary activities that don't fall in or don't admit that they fall in. . . ."

"Something of that idea," said Boon, growing a little testy—"something of that idea."

"It gives you an opportunity of annoying a number of people you don't like."

"If I offend, it is their fault!" said Boon hotly. "Criticism can have no friendships. If they like to take it ill. . . . My criticism is absolutely honest. . . . Some of them are my dearest friends."

"They won't be," said Wilkins, "when all this comes out. . . . But, anyhow, your whole case, your justification, your thesis is that there is this Mind of the Race, overriding, dominating—— And that you are its Prophet."

"Because a man confesses a belief, Wilkins, that doesn't make him a Prophet. I don't set up—I express."

"Your Mind of the Race theory has an elegance, a plausibility, I admit," said Wilkins.

Dodd's expression indicated that it didn't take him in. He compressed his lips. Not a bit of it.

"But is this in reality true? Is this what exists and goes on? We people who sit in studies and put in whole hours of our days thinking and joining things together do get a kind of coherence into our ideas about the world. Just because there is leisure and time for us to think. But are you sure that is the Race at all? That is my point. Aren't we intellectually just a by-product? If you went back to the time of Plato, you would say that the idea of his 'Republic' was what was going on in the Mind of the Race then. But I object that that was only the futile fancy of a gentleman of leisure. What was really going on was the gathering up of the Macedonian power to smash through Greece, and then make Greece conquer Asia. Your literature and philosophy are really just the private entertainment of old gentlemen out of the hurly-burly and ambitious young men too delicate to hunt or shoot. Thought is nothing in the world until it begins to operate in will and act, and the history of mankind doesn't show now, and it never has shown, any consecutive relation to human thinking. The real Mind of the Race is, I submit, something not literary at all, not consecutive, but like the inconsecutive incoherences of an idiot——"

"No," said Boon, "of a child."

"You have wars, you have great waves of religious excitement, you have patriotic and imperial delusions, you have ill-conceived and surprising economic changes——"

"As if humanity as a whole were a mere creature of chance and instinct," said Boon.

"Exactly," said Wilkins.

"I admit that," said Boon. "But my case is that sanity grows. That what was ceases to be. The mind of reason gets now out of the study into the market-place."

"You mean really, Boon, that the Mind of the Race isn't a mind that *is,* it is just a mind that becomes."

"That's what it's all about," said Boon.

"And that is where I want to take you up," said Wilkins. "I want to suggest that the Mind of the Race may be just a gleam of conscious realization that passes from darkness to darkness——"

"No," said Boon.

"Why not?"

"Because I will not have it so," said Boon. . . .

2

THERE can be no denying that from quite an early stage in the discussion Boon was excited and presently on the verge of ill-temper. This dragging of his will into a question of fact showed, I think, the beginning of his irritation. And he was short and presently rather uncivil in his replies to Wilkins.

Boon argued that behind the individualities and immediacies of life there was in reality a consecutive growth of wisdom, that larger numbers of people and a larger proportion of people than ever before were taking part in the World Mind process, and that presently this would become a great conscious general thinking of the race together.

Wilkins admitted that there had been a number of starts in the direction of impersonal understanding and explanation; indeed, there was something of the sort in every fresh religious beginning; but he argued that these starts do not show a regular progressive movement, and that none of them had ever achieved any real directive and unifying power over their adherents; that only a few Christians had ever grasped Christianity, that Brahminism fell to intellectual powder before it touched the crowd, that nowadays there was less sign than ever of the honest intellectuals getting any hold whatever upon the minds and movements of the popular mass. . . .

"The Mind of the Race," said Wilkins, "seems at times to me much more like a scared child cowering in the corner of a cage full of apes."

Boon was extraordinarily disconcerted by these contradictions.

"It will grow up," he snatched.

"If the apes let it," said Wilkins. "You can see how completely the thinkers and poets and all this stuff of literature and the study don't represent the real Mind, such as it is, of Humanity, when you note how the mass of mankind turns naturally to make and dominate its own organs of expression. Take the popular press, take the popular theatre, take popular religion, take current fiction, take the music-hall, watch the development of the cinematograph. There you have the real body of mankind expressing itself. If you are right, these things should fall in a kind of relationship to the intellectual hierarchy. But the intellectual hierarchy goes and hides away in country houses and beautiful retreats and provincial universities and stuffy high-class periodicals. It's afraid of the mass of men, it dislikes and dreads the mass of men, and it affects a pride and aloofness to cover it. Plato wanted to reorganize social order and the common life; the young man in the two-penny tube was the man he was after. He wanted to exercise him and teach him exactly what to do with the young woman beside him. Instead of which poor Plato has become just an occasion for some Oxford don to bleat about his unapproachable style and wisdom." . . .

"I admit we're not connected up yet," said Boon.

"You're more disconnected than ever you were. In the Middle Ages there was something like a connected system of ideas in Christendom, so that the Pope and the devout fishwife did in a sense march together. . . ."

You see the wrangling argument on which they were launched.

Boon maintained that there was a spreading thought process, clearly perceptible nowadays, and that those detachments of Wilkins' were not complete. He instanced the cheap editions of broad-thinking books, the variety of articles in the modern newspaper, the signs of wide discussions. Wilkins, on the other hand, asserted a predominant intellectual degeneration. . . . Moreover, Wilkins declared, with the murmurous approval of Dodd, that much even of the Academic thought process was going wrong, that Bergson's Pragmatism for Ladies was a poor substitute even for Herbert Spencer, that the boom about "Mendelism" was a triumph of weak thinking over comprehensive ideas.

"Even if we leave the masses out of account, it is still rather more than doubtful if there is any secular intellectual growth."

And it is curious to recall now that as an instance of a degenerative thought process among educated people Wilkins instanced modern Germany. Here, he said, in the case of a Mind covering over a hundred million people altogether, was a real retrocession of intellectual freedom. The pretentious expression of instinctive crudity had always been the peculiar weakness of the German mind. It had become more and more manifest, he said, as nationalism had ousted foreign influence. You see what pretty scope for mutual contradiction there was in all this. "Let me get books," cried Wilkins, "and I will read you samples of the sort of thing that passes for thinking in Germany. I will read you some of Houston Stewart Chamberlain, some of Nietzsche's boiling utterance, some of Schopenhauer.

"Let me," said Wilkins, "read a passage I have picked almost haphazard from Schopenhauer. One gets Schopenhauer rammed down one's throat as a philosopher, as a deep thinker, as the only alternative to the Hegelian dose. And just listen——"

He began to read in a voice of deliberate malice, letting his voice italicize the more scandalous transitions of what was certainly a very foolish and ill-knit piece of assertion.

"'Little men have a decided inclination for big women, and *vice versâ;* and indeed in a little man the preference for big women will be so much the more passionate if he himself was begotten by a big father, and only remains little through the influence of his mother; because he has inherited from his father the vascular system and its energy which was able to supply a large body with blood. If, on the other hand, his father and grandfather were both little, that inclination will make itself less felt. At the foundation of the aversion of a big woman to big men lies *the intention of Nature* to avoid too big a race, . . . Further, the consideration as to the complexion is very decided.

Blondes prefer dark persons or brunettes; but the latter seldom prefer the former. *The reason is,* that fair hair and blue eyes are in themselves a variation from the type, almost an abnormity, analogous to white mice, or at least to grey horses. In no part of the world, not even in the vicinity of the Pole, are they indigenous, except in Europe, and are clearly of Scandinavian origin. I may here express my opinion in passing that the white colour of the skin is not natural to man, but that by nature he has a black or brown skin, like *our forefathers the Hindus;* that consequently a white man has never originally sprung from the womb of Nature, and that thus there is no such thing as a white race, much as this is talked of, but every white man is a faded or bleached one. Forced into this strange world, where he only exists like an exotic plant, and like this requires in winter the hothouse, in the course of thousands of years man became white. The gipsies, an Indian race which immigrated only about four centuries ago, show the transition from the complexion of the Hindu to our own. *Therefore* in sexual love Nature strives to return to dark hair and brown eyes as the primitive type; but the white colour of the skin has become second nature, though not so that the brown of the Hindu repels us. Finally, each one also seeks in the particular parts of the body the corrective of his own defects and aberrations, and does so the more decidedly the more important the part is. *Therefore* snub-nosed individuals have an inexpressible liking for hook-noses, parrot-faces; and it is the same with regard to all other parts. Men with excessively slim, long bodies and limbs can find beauty in a body which is even beyond measure stumpy and short. . . . Whoever is himself in some respects very perfect does not indeed seek and love imperfection in this respect, but is yet more easily reconciled to it than others; because he himself insures the children against great imperfection of this part. For example, whoever is himself very white will not object to a yellow complexion; but whoever has the latter will find dazzling whiteness divinely beautiful.' (You will note that he perceives he has practically contradicted this a few lines before, and that evidently he has gone back and stuck in that saving clause about a white skin being second nature.) 'The rare case in which a man falls in love with a decidedly ugly woman occurs when, beside the exact harmony of the degree of sex explained above, the whole of her abnormities are precisely the opposite, and thus the corrective, of his. The love is then wont to reach a high degree.' . . .

"And so on and so on," said Wilkins. "Just a foolish, irresponsible saying of things. And all this stuff, this celibate cerebration, you must remember, is not even fresh; it was said far more funnily and pleasantly by old Campanella in his City of the Sun. And, mind you, this isn't a side issue Schopenhauer is upon; it isn't a moment of relaxation; this argument is essential to the whole argument of his philosophy." . . .

"But after all," said Boon, "Schopenhauer is hardly to be considered a modern. He was pre-Darwinian."

"Exactly why I begin with him," said Wilkins. "He was a contemporary of Darwin, and it was while Darwin was patiently and industriously building up evidence, that this nonsense, a whole torrent of it, a complete doctrine about the Will to Live, was being poured out. But what I want you to notice is that while the sort of cautious massing of evidence, the close reasoning, the honesty and veracity, that distinguished the method of Darwin and Huxley, are scarcely to be met with anywhere to-day, this spouting style of doing things is everywhere. Take any of the stuff of that intellectual jackdaw, Bernard Shaw, and you will find the Schopenhauer method in full development; caught-up ideas, glib, irrational transitions, wild assertions about the Life Force, about the effects of alcohol, about 'fear-poisoned' meat, about medical science, about economic processes, about Russia, about the Irish temperament and the English intelligence, about the thoughts and mental processes of everybody and every sort of mind, stuff too incoherent and recklessly positive ever to be systematically answered. And yet half at least of the English-speaking intelligenzia regards Shaw as a part of the thought process of the world. Schopenhauer was a pioneer in the game of impudent assertion, very properly disregarded by his own generation; Shaw's dementia samples this age. You see my case? In any rationally trained, clear-headed period Shaw would have been looked into, dissected, and disposed of long ago. . . . And here I have two other of the voices that this time respects. It is all my argument that they are respected now enormously, Boon; not merely that they exist. Men to talk and write foolishly, to make groundless positive statements and to misapprehend an opponent there have always been, but this age now tolerates and accepts them. Here is that invalid Englishman, Houston Stewart Chamberlain, who found a more congenial, intellectual atmosphere in Germany, and this is his great book, 'The Foundations of the Nineteenth Century.' This book has been received with the utmost solemnity in the highest quarters; nowhere has it been handed over to the derision which is its only proper treatment. You remember a rather readable and rather pretentious history we had in our schooldays, full of bad ethnology about Kelts and Anglo-Saxons, called J. R. Green's 'History of the English People'; it was part of that movement of professorial barbarity, of braggart race-Imperialism and anti-Irishism, of which Froude and Freeman were leaders; it smelt of Carlyle and Germany, it helped provoke the Keltic Renascence. Well, that was evidently the germ of Herr Chamberlain. Here——"

Wilkins turned over the pages.

"Here he is, in fairly good form. It is a section called 'The Turning Point,' and it's quite on all fours with Schopenhauer's 'our ancestors the Hindus.' It is part of a sketch in outline of the history of the past. 'The important thing,' he says, is to 'fix the turning-point of the history of Europe.' While he was at it he might just as well have *fixed* the equator of the history of Europe and its sparking-plug and the position of its liver. Now, listen—

"'The awakening of the Teutonic peoples to the consciousness of their all-important vocation as the founders of a completely new civilization and culture marks the turning point; the year 1200 can be designated the central moment of this awakening.'"

"Just consider that. He does not even trouble to remind us of the very considerable literature that must exist, of course, as evidence of that awakening. He just flings the statement out, knowing that his sort of follower swallows all such statements blind, and then, possibly with some qualms of doubt about what may have been happening in Spain and Italy and India and China and Japan, he goes on—

"'Scarcely any one will have the hardihood to deny that the inhabitants of Northern Europe have become the makers of the world's history. At no time have they stood alone ... others, too, have exercised influence—indeed great influence—upon the destinies of mankind, but then *always merely as opponents of the men from the north.*' ...

"Poor Jenghiz Khan, who had founded the Mogul Empire in India just about that time, and was to lay the foundations of the Yuen dynasty, and prepare the way for the great days of the Mings, never knew how *mere* his relations were with these marvellous 'men from the north.' The Tartars, it is true, were sacking Moscow somewhere about twelve hundred. . . . But let us get on to more of the recital of Teutonic glories.

"'If, however, the Teutons were not the only people who moulded the world's history' (generous admission!) 'they unquestionably' (that *unquestionably!*) 'deserve the first place; all those who appear as genuine shapers of the destinies of mankind, whether as builders of States or as discoursers of new thoughts and of original art' (oh Japan! oh Ming dynasty! oh art and life of India!) 'belong to the Teutonic race. The impulse given by the Arabs is short lived' (astronomy, chemistry, mathematics, modern science generally!); 'the Mongolians destroy but do not create anything' (Samarkand, Delhi, Pekin); 'the great Italians of the *rinascimento* were *all* born either in the north, saturated with Lombardic, Gothic, and Frankish blood, or in the extreme Germano-Hellenic south; in Spain it was the Western Goths who formed the element of life; the Jews are working out their "Renaissance" of to-day by following in every sphere as closely as possible the example of the Teutonic peoples.'

"That dodge of claiming all the great figures of the non-Teutonic nations as Teutons is carried out to magnificent extremes. Dante is a Teuton on the strength of his profile and his surname, and there is some fine play about the race of Christ. He came from Galilee, notoriously non-Jewish, and so on; but Lord Redesdale, who writes a sympathetic

Introduction, sets the seal on the Teutonic nationality of Christ by reminding us that Joseph was only the putative father. . . .

"It makes a born Teuton like myself feel his divinity," said Wilkins, and read, browsing: " 'From the moment the Teuton awakes a new world begins to open out——' Um! Um! . . . Oh, here we are again!—

" 'It is equally untrue that our culture is a renaissance of the Hellenic and the Roman; it was only after the birth of the Teutonic peoples that the renaissance of past achievements was possible and not *vice versâ.*' . . . I wonder what exactly *vice versâ* means there! . . . 'The mightiest creators of that epoch—a Shakespeare, a Michael Angelo—*do not know a word of Greek or Latin.*'

"The stalwart ignorance of it! Little Latin and less Greek even Ben Jonson allowed our William, and manifestly he was fed on Tudor translations. And the illiteracy of Michael Angelo is just an inspiration of Chamberlain's. He knows his readers. Now, in itself there is no marvel in this assertive, prejudiced,

WILKINS MAKES CERTAIN OBJECTIONS

garrulous ignorance; it is semi-sober Bierhalle chatter, written down; and, God forgive us! most of us have talked in this way at one time or another; the sign and the wonder for you, Boon, is that this stuff has been taken quite seriously by all Germany and England and America, that it is accepted as first-rank stuff, that it has never been challenged, cut up, and sent to the butterman. It is Modern Thought. It is my second sample of the contemporary Mind of the Race. And now, gentlemen, we come to the third great intellectual highkicker, Nietzsche. Nietzsche, I admit, had once a real and valid idea, and his work is built upon that real and valid idea; it is an idea that comes into the head of every intelligent person who grasps the idea of the secular change of species, the idea of Darwinism, in the course of five or six minutes after the effective grasping. This is the idea that *man is not final*. But Nietzsche was so constituted that to get an idea was to receive a revelation; this step, that every bright mind does under certain circumstances take, seemed a gigantic stride to him, a stride only possible to him, and for the rest of his lucid existence he resounded variations, he wrote epigrammatic cracker-mottoes and sham Indian apophthegms, round and about his amazing discovery. And the whole thing is summed up in the title of Dr. Alexander Tille's 'Von Darwin bis Nietzsche,' in which this miracle of the obvious, this necessary corollary, is treated as a huge advance of the mind of mankind. No one slays this kind of thing nowadays. It goes on and goes on, a perpetually reinforced torrent of unreason washing through the brain of the race. There was a time when the general intelligence would have resisted and rejected Schopenhauer, Nietzsche, Chamberlain, Shaw; now it resists such invasions less and less. That, Boon, is my case."

Wilkins, with his little pile of books for reference, his sombre manner, and his persistence, was indeed curiously suggestive of an advocate opening a trial. The Mind of the Race was far less of a continuity than it was when a generally recognized and understood orthodox Christianity held it together, as a backbone holds together the ribs and limbs and head of a body. That manifestly was what he was driving at, as Dodd presently complained. In those stabler days every one with ideas, willingly or unwillingly, had to refer to that doctrinal core, had to link up to it even if the connection was used only as a point of departure. Now more and more, as in these three examples, people began irresponsibly in the air, with rash assertions about life and race and the tendency of things. And the louder they shouted, the more fantastic and remarkable they were, the more likely they were to gather a following and establish a fresh vortex in the deliquescent confusion.

On the whole, Boon was disposed to tolerate these dispersed beginnings. "We attack truth in open order," he said, "instead of in column."

"I don't mind fresh beginnings," said Wilkins; "I don't mind open order, but I do object to blank ignorance and sheer misconception. It isn't a new beginning for Schopenhauer to say we are descended from Hindus; it is just stupidity and mental retrogression. We are no more descended from Hindus than Hindus are descended from us; that we may have a common ancestry is quite a different thing. One might as well say that the chimpanzee is descended from a gorilla or a gorilla from a chimpanzee. And it isn't any sort of truth, it is just a loud lie, that the 'Germanic' peoples realized anything whatever in the year 1200. But all these—what shall I call them? —*moderns* are more and more up to that kind of thing, stating plausible things that have already been disproved, stating things erroneously, inventing pseudo-facts, and so getting off with a flourish. In the fields of ideas, and presently in the fields of action, these wildly kicking personalities have swamped any orderly progress; they have arrested and disowned all that clearing up of thought and all that patient, triumphant arrangement of proven fact which characterized the late eighteenth and the first half of the nineteenth century. During that time the great analysis of biological science went on, which culminated in an entire revision of our conceptions of species, which opened a conceivable and hitherto undreamed-of past and future to the human imagination, which seemed to have revised and relaid the very foundations of philosophical discussion. And on that foundation, what has been done?"

"Naturally," cried Boon, "after a great achievement there must be a pause. The Mind of the Race must have its digestive interludes."

"But this is indigestion! First comes Herbert Spencer, with his misconception of the life process as a struggle of individuals to survive. His word 'Evolution' is the quintessence of the misunderstanding; his image of a steadfast, mechanical unfolding through selfishness, masked plausibly and disastrously the intricate, perplexing vision of the truth. From that sort of thing we go at a stride to the inevitable Super Man, the megatherium individual of futurity, the large egoist, and all that nonsense. Then comes a swarm of shallow, incontinent thinkers, anxious to find a simple driving force with a simple name for the whole process; the 'Life Force' and 'Will,' and so on. These things, my dear Boon, are just the appalling bubbles of gas that show how completely the Mind of the Race has failed to assimilate." . . .

"It is remarkable," said Boon, "how a metaphor may run away with the clearest of thinkers. The Mind of the Race is not so consistently gastric as all that."

"You started the metaphor," said Wilkins.

"And you mounted it and it bolted with you. To these unpleasant consequences. . . . Well, I hold, on the contrary, that after the superficialities of the sixties and seventies and eighties people's minds have been getting a firmer and firmer grip upon the reality of specific instability. The new body of intellectual experiment, which isn't indigestion at all but only a preliminary attack, is all that mass of trial thinking that one lumps together in one's mind when one speaks of Pragmatism. With the breakdown of specific boundaries the validity of the logical process beyond finite ends breaks down. We make our truth for our visible purposes as we go along, and if it does not work we make it afresh. We see life once more as gallant experiment. The boundaries of our universe recede not only in time and space but thought. The hard-and-fast line between the scientific and the poetic method disappears." . . .

"And you get Bergson," said Wilkins triumphantly.

"Bergson is of that class and type that exploits the affairs of thought. But I refuse to have Pragmatism judged by Bergson. He takes hold of the unfinished inquiries that constitute the movement of Pragmatism and he makes a soft scepticism for delicate minds with easy ways back to any old-established orthodoxy they may regret."

"But here is my case again," said Wilkins. "It is only through Bergson that the Mind of the Race, the great operating mass mind out there, can take hold of this new system of ideas." . . .

3

BUT now Boon and Wilkins were fairly launched upon a vital and entirely inconclusive controversy. Was the thought process of the world growing, spreading, progressing, or was it going to pieces? The one produced a hundred instances of the enlarging and quickening of men's minds, the other replied by instancing vulgarities, distortions, wide acceptance of nonsense. Did public advertisements make a more intelligent or less intelligent appeal now than they used to do? For half an afternoon they fought over the alleged degeneration of the *Times,* multiplying instances, comparing the "Parnellism and Crime" pamphlet with Lord Northcliffe's war indiscretions, and discussing the comparative merits of Mr. Moberly Bell's campaign to sell the twenty-year-old "Encyclopædia Britannica" and found a "Book Club" that should abolish booksellers, with the displayed and illustrated advertisements of the new period.

The talk, you see, went high and low and came to no conclusion; but I think that on the whole Wilkins did succeed in shaking Boon's half-mystical confidence in the inevitableness of human wisdom. The honours, I think, lay with Wilkins. Boon did seem to establish that in physical science there had been, and was still, a great and growing process; but he was not able to prove, he could only express his faith, that the empire of sanity was spreading to greater and more human issues. He had to fall back upon prophecy. Presently there would be another big lunge forward, and so forth. But Wilkins, on his side, was able to make a case for a steady rotting in political life, an increase in loudness, emptiness, and violence in the last twenty years: he instanced Carsonism, the methods of Tariff Reform, the vehement Feminist movement, the malignant silliness of the "rebel" Labour Press, the rankness of German "patriotism." . . .

"But there are young people thinking," said Boon at last. "It isn't just these matured showings. Where one youth thought thirty years ago, fifty are thinking now. These wild, loud things are just an irruption. Just an irruption." . . .

The mocker was distressed.

The idea of active intellectual wrongness distressed him so much that he cast aside all his detachment from Hallery, and showed plainly that to this imaginary Hallery's idea of a secular growth of wisdom in mankind he himself was quite passionately clinging. . . .

4

HE was so distressed that one day he talked about it to me alone for some time.

"Wilkins," he said, "insists on Facts. It is difficult to argue with him on that basis. You see I don't intend Hallery's view to be an induction from facts. It's a conviction, an intuition. It is not the sort of thing one perceives after reading the newspaper placards or looking at the bookshelves in the British Museum. It's something one knows for certain in the middle of the night. There is the Mind of the Race, I mean. It is something General; it is a refuge from the Particular and it is in the nature of God. That's plain, isn't it? And through it there is Communion. These phases, these irruptions are incidents. If all the world went frantic; if presently some horrible thing, some monstrous war smashed all books and thinking and civilization, still the mind would be there. It would immediately go on again and presently it would pick up all that had been done before—just as a philosopher would presently go on reading again after the servant-girl had fallen downstairs with the crockery. . . . It keeps on anyhow. . . .

"Oh! I don't know *how,* my dear fellow. I can't explain. I'm not telling you of something I've reasoned out and discovered; I'm telling you of something I *know.* It's faith if you like. It keeps on and I know it keeps on—although I can't for the life of me tell how." . . .

He stopped. He flushed.

"That, you see, is Hallery's point of view," he said awkwardly.

"But Wilkins perhaps wouldn't contradict that. His point is merely that to be exact about words, that God-Mind, that General Mind of yours, isn't exactly to be called the Mind of the Race."

"But it is the Mind of the Race," said Boon.

"It is the Mind of the Race. Most of the Race is out of touch with it, lost to it. Much of the Race is talking and doing nonsense and cruelty; astray, absurd. That does not matter to the Truth, Bliss. It matters to Literature. It matters because Literature, the clearing of minds, the release of minds, the food and guidance of minds, is the way, Literature is illumination, the salvation of ourselves and of every one from isolations." . . .

"Might be," I suggested.

"Must be," he said. "Oh! I know I've lived behind Miss Bathwick. . . . But I'm breaking out. . . . One of these days I will begin to dictate to her—and not mind what she does. . . . I'm a successful nobody—superficially—and it's only through my private thoughts and private jeering that I've come to see these things." . . .

CHAPTER VIII

THE BEGINNING OF "THE WILD ASSES OF THE DEVIL"

1

ONE day a little time after the argument with Wilkins, Boon, told me he would read me a story. He read it from a pencilled manuscript. After some anxious seeking I have found most of it again and put it together. Only a few pages are missing. Here is the story. I am sorry to say it was never finished. But he gave me a very clear conception of the contemplated end. That I will indicate in its place. And I think you will see how its idea springs from the talk with Wilkins I have had to render in the previous chapter.

2

THERE was once an Author who pursued fame and prosperity in a pleasant villa on the south coast of England. He wrote stories of an acceptable nature and rejoiced in a growing public esteem, carefully offending no one and seeking only to please. He had married under circumstances of qualified and tolerable romance a lady who wrote occasional but otherwise regular verse, he was the father of a little daughter, whose reported sayings added much to his popularity, and some of the very best people in the land asked him to dinner. He was a deputy-lieutenant and a friend of the Prime Minister, a literary knighthood was no remote possibility for him, and even the Nobel prize, given a sufficient longevity, was not altogether beyond his hopes. And this amount of prosperity had not betrayed him into any un-English pride. He remembered that manliness and simplicity which are expected from authors. He smoked pipes and not the excellent cigars he could have afforded. He kept his hair cut and never posed. He did not hold himself aloof from people of the inferior and less successful classes. He habitually travelled third class in order to study the characters he put into his delightful novels; he went for long walks and sat in inns, accosting people; he drew out his gardener. And though he worked steadily, he did not give up the care of his body, which threatened a certain plumpness and what is more to the point, a localized plumpness, not generally spread over the system but exaggerating the anterior equator. This expansion was his only care. He thought about fitness and played tennis, and every day, wet or fine, he went for at least an hour's walk. . . .

Yet this man, so representative of Edwardian literature—for it is in the region of good King Edward the story begins—in spite of his enviable achievements and prospects, was doomed to the most exhausting and dubious adventures before his life came to its unhonoured end. . . .

Because I have not told you everything about him. Sometimes—in the morning sometimes—he would be irritable and have quarrels with his shaving things, and there were extraordinary moods when it would seem to him that living quite beautifully in a pleasant villa and being well-off and famous, and writing books that were always good-humoured and grammatical and a little distinguished in an inoffensive way, was about as boring and intolerable a life as any creature with a soul to be damned could possibly pursue. Which shows only that God in putting him together had not forgotten that viscus the liver which is usual on such occasions. . . .

The winter at the seaside is less agreeable and more bracing than the summer, and there were days when this author had almost to force himself through the wholesome, necessary routine of his life, when the southwest wind savaged his villa and roared in the chimneys and slapped its windows with gustsful of rain and promised to wet that author thoroughly and exasperatingly down his neck and round his wrists and ankles directly he put his nose outside his door. And the grey waves he saw from his window came rolling inshore under the hurrying grey rain-bursts, line after line, to smash along the undercliff into vast, feathering fountains of foam and sud and send a salt-tasting spin-drift into his eyes. But manfully he would put on his puttees and his waterproof cape and his biggest brierwood pipe, and out he would go into the whurry-balloo of it all, knowing that so he would be all the brighter for his nice story-writing after tea.

On such a day he went out. He went out very resolutely along the seaside gardens of gravel and tamarisk and privet, resolved to oblige himself to go right past the harbour and up to the top of the east cliff before ever he turned his face back to the comforts of fire and wife and tea and buttered toast. . . .

And somewhere, perhaps half a mile away from home, he became aware of a queer character trying to keep abreast of him.

His impression was of a very miserable black man in the greasy, blue-black garments of a stoker, a lascar probably from a steamship in the harbour, and going with a sort of lame hobble. . . .

As he passed this individual the author had

a transitory thought of how much authors don't know in the world, how much, for instance, this shivering, cringing body might be hiding within itself, of inestimable value as "local colour" if only one could get hold of it for "putting into" one's large acceptable novels. Why doesn't one sometimes tap these sources? Kipling, for example, used to do so, with most successful results. . . . And then the author became aware that this enigma was hurrying to overtake him. He slackened his pace. . . .

The creature wasn't asking for a light; it was begging for a box of matches. And, what was odd, in quite good English.

The Author surveyed the beggar and slapped his pockets. Never had he seen so miserable a face. It was by no means a prepossessing face, with its aquiline nose, its sloping brows, its dark, deep, bloodshot eyes much too close together, its V-shaped, dishonest mouth and drenched chin-tuft. And yet it was attractively animal and pitiful. The idea flashed suddenly into the Author's head: "Why not, instead of going on, thinking emptily, through this beastly weather—why not take this man back home now, to the warm, dry study, and give him a hot drink and something to smoke, and *draw him out?*"

Get something technical and first-hand that would rather score off Kipling.

"It's damnably cold!" he shouted, in a sort of hearty, forecastle voice.

"It's worse than that," said the strange stoker.

"It's a hell of a day!" said the Author, more forcible than ever.

"Don't remind me of hell," said the stoker, in a voice of inappeasable regret.

The Author slapped his pockets again. "You've got an infernal cold. Look here, my man—confound it! would you like a hot grog?" . . .

THE WILD ASSES

3

THE scene shifts to the Author's study—a blazing coal fire, the stoker sitting dripping and steaming before it, with his feet inside the fender, while the Author fusses about the room, directing the preparation of hot drinks. The Author is acutely aware not only of the stoker but of himself. The stoker has probably never been in the home of an Author before; he is probably awe-stricken at the array of books, at the comfort, convenience, and efficiency of the home, at the pleasant personality entertaining him. . . . Meanwhile the author does not forget that the stoker is material, is "copy," is being watched, *observed*. So he poses and watches, until presently he forgets to pose in his astonishment at the thing he is observing. Because this stoker is rummier than a stoker ought to be——

He does not simply accept a hot drink; he

informs his host just how hot the drink must be to satisfy him.

"Isn't there something you could put in it—something called red pepper? I've tasted that once or twice. It's good. If you could put in a bit of red pepper."

"If you can stand that sort of thing?"

"And if there isn't much water, can't you set light to the stuff? Or let me drink it boiling, out of a pannikin or something? Pepper and all."

Wonderful fellows, these stokers! The Author went to the bell and asked for red pepper.

And then as he came back to the fire he saw something that he instantly dismissed as an optical illusion, as a mirage effect of the clouds of steam his guest was disengaging. The stoker was sitting, all crouched up, as close over the fire as he could contrive; and he was holding his black hands, not to the fire but *in* the fire, holding them pressed flat against two red, glowing masses of coal. . . . He glanced over his shoulder at the Author with a guilty start, and then instantly the Author perceived that the hands were five or six inches away from the coal.

Then came smoking. The Author produced one of his big cigars—for although a conscientious pipe-smoker himself he gave people cigars; and then, again struck by something odd, he went off into a corner of the room where a little oval mirror gave him a means of watching the stoker undetected. And this is what he saw.

He saw the stoker, after a furtive glance at him, deliberately turn the cigar round, place the lighted end in his mouth, inhale strongly, and blow a torrent of sparks and smoke out of his nose. His firelit face as he did this expressed a diabolical relief. Then very hastily he reversed the cigar again, and turned round to look at the Author. The Author turned slowly towards him.

"You like that cigar?" he asked, after one of those mutual pauses that break down a pretence.

"It's admirable."

"Why do you smoke it the other way round?"

The stoker perceived he was caught. "It's a stokehole trick," he said. "Do you mind if I do it? I didn't think you saw."

"Pray smoke just as you like," said the Author, and advanced to watch the operation.

It was exactly like the fire-eater at a village fair. The man stuck the burning cigar into his mouth and blew sparks out of his nostrils. "Ah!" he said, with a note of genuine satisfaction. And then, with the cigar still burning in the corner of his mouth, he turned to the fire and *began to rearrange the burning coals with his hands* so as to pile up a great glowing mass. He picked up flaming and white-hot lumps as one might pick up lumps of sugar. The Author watched him, dumbfounded.

"I say!" he cried. "You stokers get a bit tough."

The stoker dropped the glowing piece of

coal in his hand. "I forgot," he said, and sat back a little.

"Isn't that a bit—*extra?*" asked the Author, regarding him. "Isn't that some sort of trick?"

"We get so tough down there," said the stoker, and paused discreetly as the servant came in with the red pepper.

"Now you can drink," said the Author, and set himself to mix a drink of a pungency that he would have considered murderous ten minutes before. When he had done the stoker reached over and added more red pepper.

"I don't quite see how it is your hand doesn't burn," said the Author as the stoker drank. The stoker shook his head over the uptilted glass.

"Incombustible," he said, putting it down. "Could I have just a tiny drop more? Just brandy and pepper, if you *don't* mind. Set alight. I don't care for water except when it's super-heated steam."

And as the Author poured out another stiff

glass of this incandescent brew, the stoker put up his hand and scratched the matted black hair over his temple. Then instantly he desisted and sat looking wickedly at the Author, while the Author stared at him aghast. For at the corner of his square, high, narrow forehead, revealed for an instant by the thrusting back of the hair, a curious stumpy excrescence had been visible; and the top of his ear—he had a pointed top to his ear!

"A-a-a-a-h!" said the Author, with dilated eyes.

"A-a-a-a-h!" said the stoker, in hopeless distress.

"But you aren't——!"

"I know—I know I'm not. I know. . . . I'm a devil. A poor, lost homeless devil."

And suddenly, with a gesture of indescribable despair, the apparent stoker buried his face in his hands and burst into tears.

"Only man who's ever been decently kind to me," he sobbed. "And now—you'll chuck me out again into the beastly wet and cold.

... Beautiful fire. ... Nice drink. ... Almost homelike. ... Just to torment me. ... Boo-ooh!"

And let it be recorded to the credit of our little Author, that he did overcome his momentary horror, that he did go quickly round the table, and that he patted that dirty stoker's shoulder.

"There!" he said. "There! Don't mind my rudeness. Have another nice drink. Have a hell of a drink. I won't turn you out if you're unhappy—on a day like this. Have just a mouthful of pepper, man, and pull yourself together."

And suddenly the poor devil caught hold of his arm. "Nobody good to me," he sobbed. "Nobody good to me." And his tears ran down over the Author's plump little hand— scalding tears.

4

ALL really wonderful things happen rather suddenly and without any great emphasis upon their wonderfulness, and this was no exception to the general rule. This Author went on comforting his devil as though this was nothing more than a chance encounter with an unhappy child, and the devil let his grief and discomfort have vent in a manner that seemed at the time as natural as anything could be. He was clearly a devil of feeble character and uncertain purpose, much broken down by harshness and cruelty, and it throws a curious light upon the general state of misconception with regard to matters diabolical that it came as a quite pitiful discovery to our Author that a devil could be unhappy and heart-broken. For a long time his most earnest and persistent questioning could gather nothing except that his guest was an exile from a land of great warmth and considerable entertainment, and it was only after considerable further applications of brandy and pepper that the sobbing confidences of the poor creature grew into the form of a coherent and understandable narrative.

And then it became apparent that this person was one of the very lowest types of infernal denizen, and that his rôle in the dark realms of Dis had been that of watcher and minder of a herd of sinister beings hitherto unknown to our Author, the Devil's Wild Asses, which pastured in a stretch of meadows near the Styx. They were, he gathered, unruly, dangerous, and enterprising beasts, amenable only to a certain formula of expletives, which instantly reduced them to obedience. These expletives the stoker-devil would not repeat; to do so except when actually addressing one of the Wild Asses would, he explained, involve torments of the most terrible description. The bare thought of them gave him a shivering fit. But he gave the Author to understand that to crack these curses as one drove the Wild Asses to and from their grazing on the Elysian fields was a by no means disagreeable amusement. The assherds would try who could crack the loudest until the welkin rang.

And speaking of these things, the poor creature gave a picture of diabolical life that impressed the Author as by no means unpleasant for any one with a suitable constitution. It was like the Idylls of Theocritus done in fire; the devils drove their charges along burning lanes and sat gossiping in hedges of flames, rejoicing in the warm, dry breezes (which it seems are rendered peculiarly bracing by the faint flavour of brimstone in the air), and watching the harpies and furies and witches circling in the perpetual afterglow of that inferior sky. And ever and again there would be holidays, and one would take one's lunch and wander over the sulphur craters picking flowers of sulphur or fishing for the souls of usurers and publishers and house-agents and land-agents in the lakes of boiling pitch. It was good sport, for the usurers and publishers and house-agents and land-agents were always eager to be caught; they crowded round the hooks and fought violently for the bait, and protested vehemently and entertainingly against the Rules and Regulations that compelled their instant return to the lake of fire.

And sometimes when he was on holiday this particular devil would go through the saltpetre dunes, where the witches-brooms grow and the blasted heath is in flower, to the landing-place of the ferry whence the Great Road runs through the shops and banks of the Via Dolorosa to the New Judgement Hall, and watch the crowds of damned arriving by the steam ferry-boats of the Consolidated Charon Company. This steamboat-gazing seems about as popular down there as it is at Folkestone. Almost every day notable people arrive, and, as the devils are very well informed about terrestrial affairs—for of course all the earthly newspapers go straight to hell—whatever else could one expect? they get ovations of an almost undergraduate intensity. At times you can hear their cheering or booing, as the case may be, right away on the pastures where the Wild Asses feed. And that had been this particular devil's undoing.

He had always been interested in the career of the Rt. Hon. W. E. Gladstone. . . .

He was minding the Wild Asses. He knew the risks. He knew the penalties. But when he heard the vast uproar, when he heard the eager voices in the lane of fire saying, "It's Gladstone at last!" when he saw how quietly and unsuspiciously the Wild Asses cropped their pasture, the temptation was too much. He slipped away. He saw the great Englishman landed after a slight struggle. He joined in the outcry of "Speech! Speech!" He heard the first delicious promise of a Home Rule movement which should break the last feeble links of Celestial Control. . . .

And meanwhile the Wild Asses escaped—according to the rules and the prophecies. . . .

5

THE little Author sat and listened to this tale of a wonder that never for a moment struck him as incredible. And outside his rain-lashed window the strung-out fishing smacks pitched and rolled on their way home to Folkestone harbour. . . .

The Wild Asses escaped.

They got away to the world. And his superior officers took the poor herdsman and tried him and bullied him and passed this judgement upon him: that he must go to the earth and find the Wild Asses, and say to them that certain string of oaths that otherwise must never be repeated, and so control them and bring them back to hell. That—or else one pinch of salt on their tails. It did not matter which. One by one he must bring them back, driving them by spell and curse to the cattle-boat of the ferry. And until he had caught and brought them all back he might never return again to the warmth and comfort of his accustomed life. That was his sentence and punishment. And they put him into a shrapnel shell and fired him out among the stars, and when he had a little recovered he pulled himself together and made his way to the world.

But he never found his Wild Asses and after a little time he gave up trying.

He gave up trying because the Wild Asses, once they had got out of control, developed the most amazing gifts. They could, for instance, disguise themselves with any sort of human shape, and the only way in which they differed then from a normal human being was—according to the printed paper of instructions that had been given to their custodian when he was fired out—that "their general conduct remains that of a Wild Ass of the Devil."

"And what interpretation can we put upon *that?*" he asked the listening Author.

And there was one night in the year— Walpurgis Night, when the Wild Asses became visibly great black wild asses and kicked up their hind legs and brayed. They had to. "But then, of course," said the devil, "they would take care to shut themselves up somewhere when they felt that coming on."

Like most weak characters, the stoker devil was intensely egotistical. He was anxious to dwell upon his own miseries and discomforts and difficulties and the general injustice of his treatment, and he was careless and casually indicative about the peculiarities of the Wild Asses, the matter which most excited and interested the Author. He bored on with his doleful story, and the Author had to interrupt with questions again and again in order to get any clear idea of the situation.

The devil's main excuse for his nervelessness was his profound ignorance of human nature. "So far as I can see," he said, "they might all be Wild Asses. I tried it once——"

"Tried what?"

"The formula. You know."

"Yes?"

"On a man named Sir Edward Carson."

"Well?"

"*Ugh!*" said the devil.

"Punishment?"

"Don't speak of it. He was just a professional lawyer-politician who had lost his sense of values. . . . How was *I* to know? . . . But our people certainly know how to hurt." . . .

After that it would seem this poor devil desisted absolutely from any attempt to recover his lost charges. He just tried to live for the moment and make his earthly existence as tolerable as possible. It was clear he hated the world. He found it cold, wet, draughty. . . . "I can't understand why everybody insists upon living outside of it," he said. "If you went inside——"

He sought warmth and dryness. For a time he found a kind of contentment in charge of the upcast furnace of a mine, and then he was superseded by an electric-fan. While in this position he read a vivid account of the intense heat in the Red Sea, and he was struck by the idea that if he could get a job as stoker upon an Indian liner he might snatch some days of real happiness during that portion of the voyage. For some time his natural ineptitude prevented his realizing this project, but at last, after some bitter experiences of homelessness during a London December, he had been able to ship on an Indianward boat —only to get stranded in Folkestone in consequence of a propeller breakdown. And so here he was!

He paused.

"But about these Wild Asses?" said the Author.

The mournful, dark eyes looked at him hopelessly.

"Mightn't they do a lot of mischief?" asked the Author.

"They'll do no end of mischief," said the despondent devil.

"Ultimately you'll catch it for that?"

"Ugh!" said the stoker, trying not to think of it.

6

NOW the spirit of romantic adventure slumbers in the most unexpected places, and I have already told you of our plump Author's discontents. He had been like a smouldering bomb for some years. Now, he burst out. He suddenly became excited, energetic, stimulating, uplifting.

The Author uplifts the devil.

He stood over the drooping devil.

"But my dear chap!" he said. "You must pull yourself together. You must do better than this. These confounded brutes may be doing all sorts of mischief. While you—shirk." . . .

And so on. Real ginger.

"If I had some one to go with me. Some one who knew his way about."

The Author took whisky in the excitement of the moment. He began to move very rapidly about his room and make short, sharp gestures. You know how this sort of emotion wells up at times. "We must work from some central place," said the Author. "To begin with, London perhaps."

It was not two hours later that they started, this Author and this devil he had taken to himself, upon a mission. They went out in overcoats and warm underclothing—the Author gave the devil a thorough outfit, a double lot of Jaeger's extra thick—and they were resolved to find the Wild Asses of the Devil and send them back to hell, or at least the Author was, in the shortest possible time. In the picture you will see him with a field-glass slung under his arm, the better to watch suspected cases; in his pocket, wrapped in oiled paper, is a lot of salt to use if by chance he finds a Wild Ass when the devil and his string of oaths is not at hand. So he started. And when he had caught and done for the Wild Asses, then the Author supposed that he would come back to his nice little villa and his nice little wife, and to his little daughter who said the amusing things, and to his popularity, his large gilt-edged popularity, and—except for an added prestige—be just exactly the man he had always been. Little knowing that whosoever takes unto himself a devil and goes out upon a quest, goes out upon a quest from which there is no returning——

Nevermore.

Precipitate start of the Wild Ass hunters.

CHAPTER IX

THE HUNTING OF THE WILD ASSES OF THE DEVIL

1

AT this point the surviving manuscript comes to an abrupt end.

But Boon read or extemporized far beyond this point.

He made a figure that was at once absurd and pitiful of his little Author making this raid upon the world, resolved to detect and exorcise these suspected Wild Asses, and he told us at great length of how steadily and inevitably the poor enthusiast entangled himself in feuds and false accusations, libels and denunciations, free fights, burglaries, and so to universal execration in a perpetually tightening coil. "I'll stick to it," he squeaks, with every fresh blow of Fate. Behind him, with a developing incurable bronchitis that could never be fatal, toiled the devil, more and more despondent, more and more draggle-tailed, voiceless and unhelpful.

After a time he was perpetually trying to give his Author the slip.

But continually it is clearer that there *were* diabolical Wild Asses loose and active in the affairs of the world. . . .

One day the Author had an inspiration. "Was your lot the only lot that ever escaped?"

"Oh no!" said the devil. "Ages before—there were some. It led to an awful row. Just before the Flood. They had to be drowned out. That's why they've been so stiff with me. . . . I'm not quite sure whether they didn't interbreed. They say in hell that the world has never been quite the same place since." . . .

You see the scope this story gave Boon's disposition to derision. There were endless things that Boon hated, movements that seemed to him wanton and mischievous, outbreaks of disastrous violence, evil ideas. I should get myself into as much hot water as his Author did if I were to tell all this poor man's adventures. He went to Ulster, he pursued prominent Tariff Reformers, he started off to Mexico and came back to investigate Pan-Germanism. I seem to remember his hanging for days about the entrance to Printing House Square. . . . And there was a scene in the House of Commons. The Author and the devil had been tracking a prominent politician—never mind whom—with the growing belief that here at last they had one of them. And Walpurgis Night grew near. Walpurgis Night came.

"We must not lose sight of him," said the Author, very alert and ruthless. "If necessary we must smash the windows, blow open doors."

But the great man went down to the House as though nothing could possibly happen. They followed him.

"He will certainly rush home," said the Author, as the clock crept round to half-past eleven. "But anyhow let us get into the Strangers' Gallery and keep our eyes on him to the last."

They managed it with difficulty.

I remember how vividly Boon drew the picture for us: the rather bored House, a coming and going of a few inattentive Members, the nodding Speaker and the clerks, the silent watchers in the gallery, a little flicker of white behind the grille. And then at five minutes to twelve the honourable Member arose. . . .

"We were wrong," said the Author.

"The draught here is fearful," said the devil. "Hadn't we better go?"

The honourable Member went on speaking showy, memorable, mischievous things. The seconds ticked away. And then—then it happened.

THE WILD ASSES

The Author made a faint rattling sound in his throat and clung to the rail before him. The devil broke into a cold sweat. There, visible to all men, was a large black Wild Ass, kicking up its heels upon the floor of the House. And braying.

And nobody was minding!

The Speaker listened patiently, one long finger against his cheek. The clerks bowed over the papers. The honourable Member's two colleagues listened like men under an anæsthetic, each sideways, each with his arm over the back of the seat. Across the House one Member was furtively writing a letter and three others were whispering together.

The Author felt for the salt, then he gripped the devil's wrist.

"Say those words!" he shouted quite loudly—"say those words! Say them now. Then—we shall have him."

But you know those House of Commons ushers. And at that time their usual alertness had been much quickened by several Suffragette outrages. Before the devil had got through his second sentence or the Author could get his salt out of his pocket both devil and Author were travelling violently, scruff and pant-seat irresistibly gripped, down Saint Stephen's Hall. . . .

2

"AND you really begin to think," said Wilkins, "that there has been an increase in violence and unreasonableness in the world?"

"My case is that it is an irruption," said Boon. "But I do begin to see a sort of violence of mind and act growing in the world."

"There has always been something convulsive and extravagant in human affairs," said Wilkins. "No public thing, no collective thing, has ever had the sanity of men thinking quietly in a study."

And so we fell to discussing the Mind of the Race again, and whether there was indeed any sanity growing systematically out of human affairs, or whether this Mind of the Race was just a poor tormented rag of partial understanding that would never control the blind forces that had made and would destroy it. And it was inevitable that such a talk should presently drift to the crowning human folly, to that crowned Wild Ass of the Devil, aggressive militarism. That talk was going on, I remember, one very bright, warm, sunny day in May, or it may be in June, of 1914. And we talked of militarism as a flourish, as a kicking up of the national heels, as extravagance and waste; but, what seems to me so singular now, we none of us spoke of it or thought of it as a thing that could lead to the full horror of a universal war. Human memory is so strange and treacherous a thing that I doubt now if many English people will recall our habitual disregard in those days of war as a probability. We thought of it as a costly, foolish threatening, but that it could actually happen——!

3

SOME things are so shocking that they seem to have given no shock at all, just as there are noises that are silences because they burst the ears. And for some days after the declaration of war against Germany the whole business seemed a vast burlesque. It was incredible that this great people, for whom all Western Europe has mingled, and will to the end of time mingle, admiration with a certain humorous contempt, was really advancing upon civilization, enormously armed, scrupulously prepared, bellowing, "Deutschland, Deutschland ueber Alles!" smashing, destroying, killing. We felt for a time, in spite of reason, that it was a joke, that presently Michael would laugh. . . .

But by Jove! the idiot wasn't laughing. . . .

For some weeks nobody in the circle about Boon talked of anything but the war. The Wild Asses of the Devil became an illusion, to indicate all this that was kicking Europe to splinters. We got maps, and still more maps; we sent into the town for newspapers and got special intelligence by telephone; we repeated and discussed rumours. The Belgians were showing pluck and resource, but the French were obviously shockingly unprepared. There were weeks—one may confess it now that they have so abundantly proved the contrary—when the French seemed crumpling up like pasteboard. They were failing to save the line of the Meuse, Maubeuge, Lille, Laon; there were surrenders, there was talk of treachery, and General French, left with his flank exposed, made a costly retreat. It was one Sunday in early September that Wilkins came to us with a *Sunday Observer*. "Look," he said, "they are down on the Seine! They are sweeping right round behind the Eastern line. They have broken the French in two. Here at Senlis they are almost within sight of Paris." . . .

Then some London eavesdropper talked of

the British retreat. "Kitchener says our Army has lost half its fighting value. Our base is to be moved again from Havre to La Rochelle. . . ."

Boon sat on the edge of his hammock.

"The Germans must be beaten," he said. "The new world is killed; we go back ten thousand years; there is no light, no hope, no thought nor freedom any more unless the Germans are beaten. . . . Until the Germans are beaten there is nothing more to be done in art, in literature, in life. They are a dull, envious, greedy, cunning, vulgar, interfering, and intolerably conceited people. A world under their dominance will be intolerable. I will not live in it. . . ."

"I had never believed they would do it," said Wilkins. . . .

"Both my boys," said Dodd, "have gone into the Officers' Training Corps. They were in their cadet corps at school."

"Wasn't one an engineer?" asked Boon.

"The other was beginning to paint rather

well," said Dodd. "But it all has to stop."

"I suppose I shall have to do something," said the London eavesdropper. "I'm thirty-eight. . . . I can ride and I'm pretty fit. . . . It's a nuisance."

"What is a man of my kind to do?" asked Wilkins. "I'm forty-eight."

"I can't believe the French are as bad as they seem," said Boon. "But, anyhow, we've no business to lean on the French. . . . But I wonder now——. Pass me that map."

4

NEXT week things had mended, and the French and British were pushing the Germans back from the Marne to the Aisne. Whatever doubts we had felt about the French were dispelled in that swift week of recovery. They were all right. It was a stupendous relief, for if France had gone down, if her spirit had failed us, then we felt all liberalism, all republicanism, all freedom and light would have gone out in this world for centuries.

But then again at the Aisne the Germans stood, and our brisk rush of hope sobered down towards anxiety as the long flanking movement stretched towards the sea and the Antwerp situation developed. . . .

By imperceptible degrees our minds began to free themselves from the immediate struggle of the war, from strategy and movements, from the daily attempt to unriddle from reluctant and ambiguous dispatches, Dutch rumours, censored gaps, and uninforming maps what was happening. It became clear to us that there were to be no particular dramatic strokes, no sudden, decisive battles, no swift and clear conclusions. The struggle began to assume in our minds its true proportions, its true extent, in time, in space, in historical consequence. We had thought of a dramatic three months' conflict and a redrawn map of Europe; we perceived we were in the beginnings of a far vaster conflict; the end of an age; the slow, murderous testing and condemnation of whole systems of ideas that had bound men uneasily in communities for all our lives. We discussed—as all the world was discussing—the huge organization of sentiment and teaching that had produced this aggressive German patriotism, this tremendous national unanimity. Ford Madox Hueffer came in to tell us stories of a disciplined professoriate, of all education turned into a war propaganda, of the deliberate official mental moulding of a whole people that was at once fascinating and incredible. We went over Bernhardi and Treitschke; we weighed Nietzsche's share in that mental growth. Our talk drifted with the changing season and Boon's sudden illness after his chill, from his garden to his sitting-room, where he lay wrapped up upon a sofa, irritable and impatient with this unaccustomed experience of ill-health.

"You see how much easier it is to grow an evil weed than a wholesome plant," he said. "While this great strong wickedness has developed in Germany what thought have we had in our English-speaking community? What does our world of letters amount to? Clowns and dons and prigs, cults of the precious and cults of style, a few squeaking author-journalists and such time-serving scoundrels as I, with my patent Bathwick filter, my twenty editions, and my thousands a year. None of us with any sense of a whole community or a common purpose! Where is our strength to go against that strength of the heavy German mind? Where is the Mind of our Race?"

He looked at me with tired eyes.

"It has been a joke with us," he said.

"Is there no power of thought among free men strong enough to swing them into armies that can take this monster by the neck? Must men be bullied for ever? Are there no men to think at least as earnestly as one climbs a mountain, and to write with their uttermost pride? Are there no men to face truth as those boys at Mons faced shrapnel, and to stick for the honour of the mind and for truth and beauty as those lads stuck to their trenches? Bliss and I have tried to write of all the world of letters, and we have found nothing to write about but posturing and competition and sham reputations, and of dullness and impudence hiding and sheltering in the very sheath of the sword of thought. . . . For a little while after the war began our people seemed noble and dignified; but see now how all

Britain breaks after its first quiet into chatter about spies, sentimentality about the architecture of Louvain, invasion scares, the bitter persecution of stray Germans, and petty disputes and recriminations like a pool under a breeze. And below that nothing. While still the big thing goes on, ungrasped, day after day, a monstrous struggle of our world against the thing it will not have. . . . No one is clear about what sort of thing we will have. It is a nightmare in which we try continually to escape and have no-whither to escape. . . . What is to come out of this struggle? Just anything that may come out of it, or something we mean *shall* come out of it?"

He sat up in his bed; his eyes were bright and he had little red spots in his cheeks.

"At least the Germans stand for something. It may be brutal, stupid, intolerable, but there it is—a definite intention, a scheme of living, an order, Germanic Kultur. But what the devil do *we* stand for? Was there anything that amounted to an intellectual life at all in all our beastly welter of writing, of nice-young-man poetry, of stylish fiction and fiction without style, of lazy history, popular philosophy, slobbering criticism, Academic civilities? Is there anything here to hold a people together? Is there anything to make a new world? A literature ought to dominate the mind of its people. Yet here comes the gale, and all we have to show for our racial thought, all the fastness we have made for our souls, is a flying scud of paper scraps, poems, such poems! casual articles, whirling headlong in the air, a few novels drowning in the floods." . . .

5

THERE were times during his illness and depression when we sat about Boon very much after the fashion of Job's Comforters. And I remember an occasion when Wilkins took upon himself the responsibility for a hopeful view. There was about Wilkins's realistic sentimentality something at once akin and repugnant to Boon's intellectual mysticism, so that for a time Boon listened resentfully, and then was moved to spirited contradiction. Wilkins declared that the war was like one of those great illnesses that purge the system of a multitude of minor ills. It was changing the spirit of life about us; it would end a vast amount of mere pleasure-seeking and aimless extravagance; it was giving people a sterner sense of duty and a more vivid apprehension of human brotherhood. This ineffective triviality in so much of our literary life of which Boon complained would give place to a sense of urgent purpose. . . .

"War," said Boon, turning his face towards Wilkins, "does nothing but destroy."

"All making is destructive," said Wilkins, while Boon moved impatiently; "the sculptor destroys a block of marble, the painter scatters a tube of paint. . . ."

Boon's eye had something of the expression of a man who watches another ride his favourite horse.

"See already the new gravity in people's faces, the generosities, the pacification of a thousand stupid squabbles——"

"If you mean Carsonism," said Boon, "it's only sulking until it can cut in again."

"I deny it," said Wilkins, warming to his faith. "This is the firing of the clay of Western European life. It stops our little arts perhaps—but see the new beauty that comes. . . . We can well spare our professional books and professional writing for a time to get such humour and wonder as one can find in the soldiers' letters from the front. Think of all the people whose lives would have been slack and ignoble from the cradle to the grave, who are being twisted up now to the stern question of enlistment; think of the tragedies of separation and danger and suffering that are throwing a stern bright light upon ten thousand obscure existences." . . .

"And the noble procession of poor devils tramping through the slush from their burning homes, God knows whither! And the light of fire appearing through the cracks of falling walls, and charred bits of old people in the slush of the roadside, and the screams of men disembowelled, and the crying of a dying baby in a wet shed full of starving refugees who do not know whither to go. Go on, Wilkins."

"Oh, if you choose to dwell on the horrors——!"

"The one decent thing that we men who sit at home in the warm can do is to dwell on the horrors and do our little best to make sure that never, never shall this thing happen again. And that won't be done, Wilkins, by leaving War alone. War, war with modern machines, is a damned great horrible trampling monster, a filthy thing, an indecency; we aren't doing anything heroic, we are trying to lift a foul stupidity off the earth, we are engaged in a colossal sanitary job. These men who go for us into the trenches, they come back with no illusions. They know how dirty and monstrous it is. They are like men who have gone down for the sake of the people they love to clear out a choked drain. They have no illusions about being glorified. They only hope they aren't blood-poisoned and their bodies altogether ruined. And as for the bracing stir of it, they tell me, Wilkins, that their favourite song now in the trenches is—

> "'Nobody knows how bored we are,
> Bored we are,
> Bored we are,
> Nobody knows how bored we are,
> And nobody seems to care.'

Meanwhile you sit at home and feel vicariously ennobled."

He laid his hand on a daily newspaper beside him.

"Oh, you're not the only one. I will make you ashamed of yourself, Wilkins. Here's the superlative to your positive. Here's the sort of man I should like to hold for five minutes head downwards in the bilge of a trench, writing on the Heroic Spirit in the *Morning Post*. He's one of your gentlemen who sit in a room full of books and promise themselves much moral benefit from the bloodshed in France. Coleridge, he says, Coleridge—the heroic, self-controlled Spartan Coleridge was of his opinion and very hard on Pacificism—Coleridge complained of peace time in such words as these: 'All individual dignity and power, engulfed in courts, committees, institutions. . . . One benefit-club for mutual flattery.' . . . And then, I suppose, the old loafer went off to sponge on somebody. . . . And here's the stuff the heroic, spirited Osborn, the *Morning Post* gentleman—unhappily not a German, and unhappily too old for trench work—quotes with delight now—*now!*—after Belgium!—

> "'My spear, my sword, my shaggy shield!
> With these I till, with these I sow,
> With these I reap my harvest field—
> No other wealth the gods bestow:
> With these I plant the fertile vine,
> With these I press the luscious wine.
>
> My spear, my sword, my shaggy shield!
> They make me lord of all below—
> For those who dread my spear to wield,
> Before my shaggy shield must bow.
> Their fields, their vineyards, they resign,
> And all that cowards have is mine.'

"He goes on to this—

"'It is in vain that the Pacificist rages at such staunch braggadocio. It blares out a political truth of timeless validity in words that are by no means politic. Sparta was the working model in ancient times of the State that lives by and for warfare, though never despising the rewards of an astute diplomacy; she was the Prussia of antiquity. . . .

"'Spartan ideal of duty and discipline.'. . .

"You see the spirit of him! You see what has got loose! It is a real and potent spirit; you have to reckon with it through all this business. To this sort of mind the 'Pacificist' is a hateful fool. The Pacificist prefers making vineyards, painting pictures, building Gothic cathedrals, thinking clear thoughts to bawling 'Bruteland, Bruteland, over all!' and killing people and smashing things up. He is a maker. That is what is intended here by a 'coward.' All real creative activity is hateful to a certain ugly, influential, aggressive type of mind, to this type of mind that expresses itself here in England through the *Morning Post* and *Spectator*. Both these papers are soaked through and through with a genuine detestation of all fine creation, all beauty, all novelty, all frank, generous, and pleasant things. In peace-time they maintain an attitude of dyspeptic hostility to free art, to free literature, to fresh thought. They stand uncompromisingly for ugliness, dullness, and restriction—as ends in themselves. When you talk, Wilkins, of the intellectual good of the war, I ask you to note the new exultation that has come into these evil papers. When they speak of the 'moral benefits' of war they mean the smashing up of everything that they hate and we care for. They mean reaction. This good man Osborn, whom I have never seen or heard of before, seems to be quintessential of all that side. I can imagine him. I believe I could reconstruct him from this article I have here, just as anatomists have reconstructed extinct monsters from a single bone. He is, I am certain, a don. The emotional note suggests Oxford. He is a classical scholar. And that is the extent of his knowledge. Something in this way."

He began to sketch rapidly.

THE WILD ASSES

Fancy portrait of Mr. E. B. Osborn, singing about his sword and his shield and his ruthless virility, and all that sort of thing.

"You have to realize that while the Pacificists talk of the horrible ugliness of war and the necessity of establishing an everlasting world-peace, whiskered old ladies in hydropaths, dons on the *Morning Post,* chattering district visitors and blustering, bellowing parsons, people who are ever so much more representative of general humanity than we literary oddities—all that sort of people tucked away somewhere safe, are in a state of belligerent lustfulness and prepared—oh, prepared to give the very eyes of everybody else in this country, prepared to sacrifice the lives of all their servants and see the poor taxed to the devil, first for a victory over Germany and then for the closest, silliest, loudest imitation of Prussian swagger on our part (with them, of course, on the very top of it all) that we can contrive. That spirit is loose, Wilkins. All the dowagers are mewing for blood, all the male old women who teach classics and dream of re-action at Oxford and Cambridge, are having the time of their lives. They trust to panic, to loud accusations, to that fear of complexity that comes with fatigue. They trust to the exhaustion of delicate purposes and sensitive nerves. And this force-loving, bullying silliness is far more likely to come out on top, after the distresses of this war, after the decent men are dead in the trenches and the wise ones shouted to silence, than any finely intellectual, necessarily difficult plan to put an end for ever to all such senseless brutalities."

"I think you underrate the power of—well, modern sanity," said Wilkins.

"Time will show," said Boon. "I hope I do."

"This man Osborn, whoever he may be, must be just a fantastic extremist. . . . I do not see that he is an answer to my suggestion that for the whole mass of people this war means graver thought, steadier thought, a firmer collective purpose. It isn't only by books and formal literature that people think. There is the tremendous effect of realized and accumulated facts——"

"Wilkins," said Boon, "do not cuddle such illusions. It is only in books and writings that facts get assembled. People are not grasping any comprehensive effects at all at the present time. One day one monstrous thing batters on our minds—a battleship is blown up or a hundred villagers murdered—and next day it is another. We do not so much think about it as get mentally scared. . . . You can see in this spy hunt that is going on and in the increasing denunciations and wrangling of the papers how the strain is telling. . . . Attention is overstrained and warms into violence. People are reading no books. They are following out no conclusions. No intellectual force whatever is evident dominating the situation. No organization is at work for a sane peace. Where is any *power* for Pacificism? Where is any strength on its side? America is far too superior to do anything but trade, the liberals here sniff at each other and quarrel gently but firmly on minor points, Mr. Norman Angell advertises himself in a small magazine and resents any other work for peace as though it were an infringement of his copyright. Read the daily papers; go and listen to the talk of people! Don't theorize, but watch. The mind you will meet is not in the least like a mind doing something slowly but steadfastly; far more is it like a mind being cruelly smashed about and worried and sticking to its immediate purpose with a narrower and narrower intensity. Until at last it is a pointed intensity. It is like a dying man strangling a robber in his death-grip. . . .

We shall beat them, but we shall be dead beat doing it. . . . You see, Wilkins, I have tried to think as you do. In a sort of way this war has inverted our relations. I say these things now because they force themselves upon me." . . .

Wilkins considered for some moments.

"Even if nothing new appears," he said at last, "the mere beating down and discrediting of the militarist system leaves a world released." . . .

"But will it be broken down?" said Boon. "Think of the Osborns."

And then he cried in a voice of infinite despair: "No! War is just the killing of things and the smashing of things. And when it is all over, then literature and civilization will have to begin all over again. They will have to begin lower down and against a heavier load, and the days of our jesting are done. The Wild Asses of the Devil are loose and there is no restraining them. What is the good, Wilkins, of pretending that the Wild Asses are the instruments of Providence kicking better than we know? It is all evil. Evil. An evil year. And I lie here helpless, spitting and spluttering, with this chill upon my chest. . . . I cannot say or write what I would. . . . And in the days of my sunshine there were things I should have written, things I should have understood." . . .

6

AFTERWARDS Boon consoled himself very much for a time by making further speculative sketches of Mr. Osborn, as the embodiment of the Heroic Spirit. I append one or two of the least offensive of these drawings.

Fancy sketch of Mr. Osborn (the Heroic Spirit) compelling his tailor to make him trousers for nothing.

*My weapon with my tailor speaks,
It cuts my coat and sews my breeks.*

THE WILD ASSES

Mr. Osborn, in a moment of virile indignation, swiping St. Francis of Assisi one with a club.

The soul of Mr. Osborn doing a war dance (as a Spartan Red Indian) in order to work itself up for a "Morning Post" article.

THE WILD ASSES

Mr. Osborn's dream of himself as a Prussian Spartan refreshing himself with Hero's food (fresh human liver) and drink (blood and champagne) after a good Go In at some Pacificist softs.

7

BOON'S pessimistic outlook on the war had a profoundly depressing effect upon me. I do all in my power to believe that Wilkins is right, and that the hopelessness that darkened Boon's last days was due to the overshadowing of his mind by his illness. It was not simply that he despaired of the world at large; so far as I am concerned, he pointed and barbed his opinion by showing how inevitable it was that the existing publishing and book trade would be shattered to fragments. Adapted as I am now to the necessities of that trade, incapable as I am of the fresh exertions needed to bring me into a successful relationship to the unknown exigencies of the future, the sense of complete personal ruin mingled with and intensified the vision he imposed upon me of a world laid waste. I lay awake through long stretches of the night contemplating now my own life, no longer in its first vigour, pinched by harsh necessities and the fiercer competition of a young and needy generation, and now all life with its habits and traditions strained and broken. My daily fatigues at drill and the universal heavy cold in the head that has oppressed all Britain this winter almost more than the war, have added their quota to my nightly discomfort. And when at last I have slept I have been oppressed with peculiar and melancholy dreams.

One is so vividly in my mind that I am obliged to tell it here, although I am doubtful whether, except by a very extreme stretching of the meaning of words, we can really consider it among the Remains of George Boon.

It was one of those dreams of which the scenery is not so much a desolate place as desolation itself, and I was there toiling up great steepnesses with a little box of something in my hand. And I knew, in that queer confused way that is peculiar to dreams, that I was not myself but that I was the Author who is the hero of the Wild Asses of the Devil, and also that I was neither he nor I, but all sorts of authors, the spirit of authorship, no Author in particular but the Author at large, and that, since the melancholy devil had deserted me— he had sneaked off Heaven knows whither—it rested with me and with me alone to discover and catch and send out of this tormented world those same Wild Asses of the Devil of which you have read. And so I had salt in my box, Attic Salt, a precious trust, the one thing in all the universe with which I could subdue them.

And then suddenly there I was amidst all those very asses of which I have told you. There they were all about me, and they were more wild and horrible than I can describe to you. It was not that they were horrible in any particular way, they were just horrible, and they kicked up far overhead, and leapt and did not even seem to trouble to elude my poor ineffectual efforts to get within salting distance of them. I toiled and I pursued amidst mad mountains that were suddenly marble flights of stairs that sloped and slid me down to precipices over which I floated; and then we were in soft places knee-deep in blood-red mud; and then they were close to my face, eye to eye, enormous revolving eyes, like the lanterns of lighthouses; and then they swept away, and always I grew smaller and feebler and more breathless, and always they grew larger, until only their vast legs danced about me on the sward, and all the rest was hidden. And all the while I was tugging at my box of Attic Salt, to get it open, to get a pinch. Suddenly I saw they were all coming down upon me, and all the magic salt I had was in the box that would not open. . . .

I saw the sward they trampled, and it was not sward, it was living beings, men hurt by dreadful wounds, and poor people who ran in streaming multitudes under the beating hoofs, and a lichenous growth of tender things and beautiful and sweet and right things on which they beat, splashing it all to blood and dirt. I could not open my box. I could not open my box. And a voice said: "Your box! Your box! Laugh at them for the fools they are, and at the salt sting of laughter back they will fly to hell!"

But I could not open my box, for I thought of my friend's sons and dear friends of my own, and there was no more spirit in me. "We cannot laugh!" I cried. "We cannot laugh! Another generation! Another generation may have the heart to do what we cannot do."

And the voice said: "Courage! Only your poor courage can save us!"

But in my dream I could do no more than weep pitifully and weep, and when I woke up my eyes were wet with tears.

CHAPTER X

THE STORY OF THE LAST TRUMP

1

"AFTER this war," said Wilkins, "after its revelation of horrors and waste and destruction, it is impossible that people will tolerate any longer that system of diplomacy and armaments and national aggression that has brought this catastrophe upon mankind. This is the war that will end war."

"Osborn," said Boon, "Osborn."

"But after all the world has seen——!"

"The world doesn't see," said Boon. . . .

Boon's story of the Last Trump may well come after this to terminate my book. It has been by no means an easy task to assemble the various portions of this manuscript. It is written almost entirely in pencil, and sometimes the writing is so bad as to be almost illegible. But here at last it is, as complete, I think, as Boon meant it to be. It is his epitaph upon his dream of the Mind of the Race.

2

THE story of the Last Trump begins in heaven, and it ends in all sorts of places round about the world.

Heaven, you must know, is a kindly place, and the blessed ones do not go on forever singing Alleluia, whatever you may have been told. For they, too, are finite creatures, and must be fed with their eternity in little bits, as one feeds a chick or a child. So there are mornings and changes and freshness, there is time to condition their lives. And the children are still children, gravely eager about their playing and ready always for new things; just children they are, but blessèd as you see them in the pictures beneath the careless feet of the Lord God. And one of these blessèd children routing about in an attic—for Heaven is, of course, full of the most heavenly attics, seeing that it has children—came upon a number of instru-

[303]

ments stored away, and laid its little chubby hands upon them. . . .

Now, indeed, I cannot tell what these instruments were, for to do so would be to invade mysteries. . . . But one I may tell of, and that was a great brazen trumpet which the Lord God had made when He made the world —for the Lord God finishes all His jobs—to blow when the time for our Judgement came round. And He had made it and left it; there it was, and everything was settled exactly as the Doctrine of Predestination declares. And this blessèd child conceived one of those unaccountable passions of childhood for its smoothness and brassiness, and he played with it and tried to blow it, and trailed it about with him out of the attic into the gay and golden streets, and, after many fitful wanderings, to those celestial battlements of crystal of which you have doubtless read. And there the blessèd child fell to counting the stars, and forgot all about the trumpet beside him until a flourish of his elbow sent it over.

Down fell the trump, spinning as it fell, and for a day or so, which seemed but moments in heaven, the blessèd child watched its fall until it was a glittering little speck of brightness. . . .

When it looked a second time the trump was gone. . . . I do not know what happened to that child when at last it was time for Judgement Day and that shining trumpet was missed. I know that Judgement Day is long overpassed, because of the wickedness of the world; I think perhaps it was in 1000 A. D. when the expected Day should have dawned that never came, but no other heavenly particulars do I know at all, because now my scene changes to the narrow ways of this Earth. . . . And the Prologue in Heaven ends.

3

AND now the scene is a dingy little shop in Caledonian Market, where things of an incredible worthlessness lie in wait for such as seek after an impossible cheapness. In the window, as though it had always been there and never anywhere else, lies a long, battered, discoloured trumpet of brass that no prospective purchaser has ever been able to sound. In it mice shelter, and dust and fluff have gathered after the fashion of this world. The keeper of the shop is a very old man, and he bought the shop long ago, but already this trumpet was there; he has no idea whence it came, nor its country or origin, nor anything about it. But once in a moment of enterprise that led to nothing he decided to call it an Ancient Ceremonial Shawm, though he ought to have known that whatever a shawm may be the last thing it was likely to be is a trumpet, seeing that they are always mentioned together.

And above it hung concertinas and melodeons and cornets and tin whistles and mouth-organs and all that rubbish of musical instruments which delight the hearts of the poor. Until one day two blackened young men from the big motor works in the Pansophist Road stood outside the window and argued.

They argued about these instruments in stock and how you made these instruments sound, because they were fond of argument, and one asserted and the other denied that he could make every instrument in the place sound a note. And the argument rose high, and led to a bet.

"Supposing, of course, that the instrument is in order," said Hoskin, who was betting he could.

"That's understood," said Briggs.

And then they called as witnesses certain other young and black and greasy men in the same employment, and after much argument and discussion that lasted through the afternoon, they went in to the little old dealer about tea-time, just as he was putting a blear-eyed, stinking paraffin-lamp to throw an unfavorable light upon his always very unattractive window. And after great difficulty they arranged that for the sum of one shilling, paid in advance, Hoskin should have a try at every instrument in the shop that Briggs chose to indicate.

And the trial began.

The third instrument that was pitched upon by Briggs for the trial was the strange trumpet that lay at the bottom of the window, the trumpet that you, who have read the Introduction, know was the trumpet for the Last Trump. And Hoskin tried and tried again, and then, blowing desperately, hurt his ears. But he could get no sound from the trumpet. Then he examined the trumpet more carefully and discovered the mice and fluff and other things in it, and demanded that it should be cleaned; and the old dealer, nothing loath, knowing they were used to automobile-horns and such-like instruments, agreed to let them clean it on condition that they left it shiny. So the young men, after making a suitable deposit,—which, as you shall hear, was presently confiscated,— went off with the trumpet, proposing to clean it next day at the works and polish it with the peculiarly excellent brass polish employed upon the honk-honk horns of the firm. And this they did, and Hoskin tried again.

But he tried in vain. Whereupon there arose a great argument about the trumpet, whether it was in order or not, whether it was possible for any one to sound it. For if not, then clearly it was outside the condition of the bet.

Others among the young men tried it, including two who played wind instruments in a band and were musically knowing men. After their own failure they were strongly on the side of Hoskin and strongly against Briggs, and most of the other young men were of the same opinion.

"Not a bit of it," said Briggs, who was a

man of resource. "*I*'ll show you that it can be sounded."

And taking the instrument in his hand, he went toward a peculiarly powerful foot blow-pipe that stood at the far end of the tool-shed. "Good old Briggs!" said one of the other young men, and opinion veered about.

Briggs removed the blow-pipe from its bellows and tube, and then adjusted the tube very carefully to the mouthpiece of the trumpet. Then with great deliberation he produced a piece of beeswaxed string from a number of other strange and filthy contents in his pocket, and tied the tube to the mouthpiece. And then he began to work the treadle of the bellows.

"Good old Briggs!" said the one who had previously admired him.

And then something incomprehensible happened.

It was a flash. Whatever else it was it was a flash. And a sound that seemed to coincide exactly with the flash.

Afterward the young men agreed to it that the trumpet blew to bits. It blew to bits and vanished, and they were all flung upon their faces—not backward, be it noted, but on their faces—and Briggs was stunned and scared. The tool-shed windows were broken and the various apparatus and cars around were much displaced, and *no traces of the trumpet were ever discovered.*

That last particular puzzled and perplexed poor Briggs very much. It puzzled and perplexed him the more because he had had an impression so extraordinary, so incredible, that he was never able to describe it to any other living person. But his impression was this: that the flash that came with the sound came not from the trumpet, but to it, that it smote down to it and took it, and that its shape was in the exact likeness of a hand and arm of fire.

4

AND that was not all; that was not the only strange thing about the disappearance of that battered trumpet. There was something else even more difficult to describe, an effect as though for one instant something opened.

The young men who worked with Hoskin and Briggs had that clearness of mind which comes of dealing with machinery, and all felt this indescribable something else, as if for an instant the world was not the world, but something lit and wonderful, larger.

This is what one of them said of it.

"I felt," he said, "just for a minute as though I was blown to kingdom come."

"It is just how it took me," said another. " 'Lord,' I says, 'here's Judgement Day!' and there I was sprawling among the files. . . ."

But none of the others felt that he could say anything more definite than that.

5

MOREOVER, there was a storm. All over the world there was a storm that puzzled meteorology, a moment's gale that left the atmosphere in a state of wild commotion, rains, tornadoes, depressions, irregularities for weeks. News came of it from all the quarters of the earth.

All over China, for example, that land of cherished graves, there was a dust-storm; dust leaped into the air. A kind of earthquake shook Europe—an earthquake that seemed to have at heart the peculiar interests of Mr. Algernon Ashton: everywhere it cracked mausoleums and shivered the pavements of cathedrals, swished the flower-beds of cemeteries, and tossed tombstones aside. A crematorium in Texas blew up. The sea was greatly agitated, and the beautiful harbour of Sydney, in Australia, was seen to be littered with sharks floating upside down in manifest distress.

And all about the world a sound was heard like the sound of a trumpet instantly cut short.

6

BUT this much is only the superficial dressing of the story. The reality is something different. It is this: that in an instant, and for an instant, the dead lived, and all that are alive in the world did for a moment see the Lord God and all His powers, His hosts of angels, and all His array looking down upon them. They saw Him as one sees by a flash of lightning in the darkness, and then instantly the world was opaque again, limited, petty, habitual. That is the tremendous reality of this story. Such glimpses have happened in individual cases before. The lives of the saints abound in them. Such a glimpse it was that came to Rabindranath Tagore upon the burning ghat at Benares. But this was not an individual but a world experience; the flash came to every one. Not always was it quite the same, and thereby the doubter found his denials when presently a sort of discussion broke out in the obscurer Press. For this one testified that it seemed that "One stood very near to me," and another saw "all the hosts of heaven flame up toward the Throne."

And there were others who had a vision of brooding watchers, and others who imagined great sentinels before a veiled figure, and some one who felt nothing more divine than a sensation of happiness and freedom such as one gets from a sudden burst of sunshine in the spring. . . . So that one is forced to believe that something more than wonderfully wonderful, something altogether strange, was seen, and that all these various things that people thought they saw were only interpretations drawn from their experiences and their imaginations. It was a light, it was beauty, it was high and solemn, it made this world seem a flimsy transparency. . . .

Then it had vanished. . . .

And people were left with the question of what they had seen, and just how much it mattered.

7

A LITTLE old lady sat by the fire in a small sitting-room in West Kensington. Her cat was in her lap, her spectacles were on her nose; she was reading the morning's paper, and beside her, on a little occasional table, was her tea and a buttered muffin. She had finished the crimes and she was reading about the Royal Family. When she had read all there was to read about the Royal Family, she put down the paper, deposited the cat on the hearth-rug, and turned to her tea. She had poured out her first cup and she had just taken up a quadrant of muffin when the trump and the flash came. Through its instant duration she remained motionless with the quadrant of muffin poised halfway to her mouth. Then very slowly she put the morsel down.

"Now, what was that?" she said.

She surveyed the cat, but the cat was quite

calm. Then she looked very, very hard at her lamp. It was a patent safety-lamp, and had always behaved very well. Then she stared at the window, but the curtains were drawn, and everything was in order.

"One might think I was going to be ill," she said, and resumed her toast.

8

NOT far away from this old lady, not more than three-quarters of a mile at most, sat Mr. Parchester in his luxurious study, writing a perfectly beautiful, sustaining sermon about the Need of Faith in God. He was a handsome, earnest, modern preacher, he was rector of one of our big West End churches, and he had amassed a large, fashionable congregation. Every Sunday, and at convenient intervals during the week, he fought against Modern Materialism, Scientific Education, Excessive Puritanism, Pragmatism, Doubt, Levity, Selfish Individualism, Further Relaxation of the Divorce Laws, all the Evils of our Time— and anything else that was unpopular. He believed quite simply, he said, in all the old, simple, kindly things. He had the face of a saint, but he had rendered this generally acceptable by growing side-whiskers. And nothing could tame the beauty of his voice.

He was an enormous asset in the spiritual life of the metropolis—to give it no harsher name—and his fluent periods had restored faith and courage to many a poor soul hovering on the brink of the dark river of thought. . . .

And just as beautiful Christian maidens played a wonderful part in the last days of Pompeii, in winning proud Roman hearts to a hated and despised faith, so Mr. Parchester's naturally graceful gestures, and his simple, melodious, trumpet voice won back scores of our half-pagan rich women to church attendance and the social work of which his church was the centre. . . .

And now by the light of an exquisitely shaded electric lamp he was writing this sermon of quiet, confident belief (with occasional hard smacks, perfect stingers in fact, at current unbelief and rival leaders of opinion), in the simple, divine faith of our fathers. . . .

When there came this truncated trump and this vision. . . .

9

OF all the innumerable multitudes who for the infinitesimal fraction of a second had this glimpse of the Divinity, none were so blankly and profoundly astonished as Mr. Parchester. For—it may be because of his subtly spiritual nature—he *saw,* and seeing believed. He dropped his pen and let it roll across his manuscript, he sat stunned, every drop of blood fled from his face and his lips and his eyes dilated.

While he had just been writing and arguing about God, there *was* God!

The curtain had been snatched back for an instant. It had fallen again; but his mind had taken a photographic impression of everything that he had seen—the grave presences, the hierarchy, the effulgence, the vast concourse, the terrible, gentle eyes. He felt it, as though the vision still continued, behind the bookcases, behind the pictured wall and the curtained window: *even now there was judgement!*

For quite a long time he sat, incapable of more than apprehending this supreme realization. His hands were held out limply upon the desk before him. And then very slowly his staring eyes came back to immediate things, and fell upon the scattered manuscript on which he had been engaged. He read an unfinished sentence and slowly recovered its intention. As he did so, a picture of his congregation came to him as he saw it from the pulpit during his evening sermon, as he had intended to see it on the Sunday evening that was at hand, with Lady Rupert in her sitting and Lady Blex in hers and Mrs. Munbridge, the rich and in her Jewish way very attractive Mrs. Munbridge, running them close in her adoration, and each with one or two friends they had brought to adore him, and behind them the Hexhams and the Wassinghams and behind them others and others and others, ranks and ranks of people, and the galleries on either side packed with worshippers of a less dominant class, and the great organ and his magnificent choir waiting to support him and supplement him, and the great altar to the left of him, and the beautiful new Lady Chapel, done by Roger Fry and Wyndham Lewis and all the latest people in art, to the right. He thought of the listening multitude, seen through the haze of the thousand electric candles, and how he had planned the paragraphs of his discourse so that the notes of his beautiful voice should float slowly down, like golden leaves in autumn, into the smooth tarn of their silence, word by word, phrase by phrase, until he came to—

"Now to God the Father, God the Son——"

And all the time he knew that Lady Blex would watch his face and Mrs. Munbridge, leaning those graceful shoulders of hers a little forward, would watch his face. . . .

Many people would watch his face.

All sorts of people would come to Mr. Parchester's services at times. Once it was said Mr. Balfour had come. Just to hear him. After his sermons, the strangest people would come and make confessions in the beautifully furnished reception-room beyond the vestry. All sorts of people. Once or twice he had asked people to come and listen to him; and one of them had been a very beautiful woman. And often he had dreamt of the people who might come: prominent people, influential people, remarkable people. But never before had it occurred to Mr. Parchester that, a little hidden from the rest of the congregation, behind the thin veil of this material world, there was another auditorium. And that God also, God also, watched his face.

And watched him through and through.

Terror seized upon Mr. Parchester.

He stood up, as though Divinity had come into the room before him. He was trembling. He felt smitten and about to be smitten.

He perceived that it was hopeless to try to hide what he had written, what he had thought, the unclean egotism he had become.

"I did not know," he said at last.

The click of the door behind him warned him that he was not alone. He turned, and saw Miss Skelton, his typist, for it was her time to come for his manuscript and copy it out in the specially legible type he used. For a moment he stared at her strangely.

She looked at him with those deep, adoring eyes of hers. "Am I too soon, sir?" she asked in her slow, unhappy voice, and seemed prepared for a noiseless departure.

He did not answer immediately. Then he said: "Miss Skelton, the Judgement of God is close at hand!"

And seeing she stood perplexed, he said—

"Miss Skelton, how can you expect me to go on acting and mouthing this Tosh when the Sword of Truth hangs over us?"

Something in her face made him ask a question.

"Did *you* see anything?" he asked.

"I thought it was because I was rubbing my eyes."

"Then indeed there is a God! And He is

watching us now. And all this about us, this sinful room, this foolish costume, this preposterous life of blasphemous pretension——!"

He stopped short, with a kind of horror on his face.

With a hopeless gesture he rushed by her. He appeared wild-eyed upon the landing before his man-servant, who was carrying a scuttle of coal up-stairs.

"Brompton," he said, "what are you doing?"

"Coal, sir."

"Put it down, man!" he said. "Are you not an immortal soul? God is here! As close as my hand! Repent! Turn to Him! The Kingdom of Heaven is at hand!"

10

NOW if you are a policeman perplexed by a sudden and unaccountable collision between a taxicab and an electric standard, complicated by a blinding flash and a sound like an abbreviated trump from an automobile horn, you do not want to be bothered by a hatless clerical gentleman suddenly rushing out of a handsome private house and telling you that "the Kingdom of Heaven is at hand!" You are respectful to him because it is the duty of a policeman to be respectful to gentlemen, but you say to him, "Sorry I can't attend to that now, sir. One thing at a time. I've got this little accident to see to." And if he persists in dancing round the gathering crowd and coming at you again, you say: "I'm afraid I must ask you just to get away from here, sir. You aren't being an 'elp, sir." And if, on the other hand, you are a well-trained clerical gentleman, who knows his way about in the world, you do not go on pestering a policeman on duty after he has said that, even although you think God is looking at you and Judgement is close at hand. You turn away and go on, a little damped, looking for some one else more likely to pay attention to your tremendous tidings.

And so it happened to the Reverend Mr. Parchester.

He experienced a curious little recession of confidence. He went on past quite a number of people without saying anything further, and the next person he accosted was a flower-woman sitting by her basket at the corner of Chexington Square. She was unable to stop him at once when he began to talk to her because she was tying up a big bundle of white chrysanthemums and had an end of string behind her teeth. And her daughter who stood beside her was the sort of girl who wouldn't say "Bo!" to a goose.

"Do you know, my good woman," said Mr. Parchester, "that while we poor creatures of

THE STORY OF THE LAST TRUMP

earth go about our poor business here, while we sin and blunder and follow every sort of base end, close to us, above us, around us, watching us, judging us, are God and His holy angels? I have had a vision, and I am not the only one. I have *seen*. We are *in* the Kingdom of Heaven now and here, and Judgement is all about us now! Have you seen nothing? No light? No sound? No warning?"

By this time the old flower-seller had finished her bunch of flowers and could speak. "I saw it," she said. "And Mary—she saw it."

"Well?" said Mr. Parchester.

"But, Lord! It don't *mean* nothing!" said the old flower-seller.

11

AT that a kind of chill fell upon Mr. Parchester. He went on across Chexington Square by his own inertia.

He was still about as sure that he had seen God as he had been in his study, but now he was no longer sure that the world would believe that he had. He felt perhaps that this idea of rushing out to tell people was precipitate and inadvisable. After all, a priest in the Church of England is only one unit in a great machine; and in a world-wide spiritual crisis it should be the task of that great machine to act as one resolute body. This isolated crying aloud in the street was unworthy of a consecrated priest. It was a dissenting kind of thing to do. A vulgar individualistic screaming. He thought suddenly that he would go and tell his bishop—the great Bishop Wampach. He called a taxicab, and within half an hour he was in the presence of his commanding officer. It was an extraordinarily difficult and painful interview. . . .

You see, Mr. Parchester believed. The Bishop impressed him as being quite angrily resolved not to believe. And for the first time in his career Mr. Parchester realized just how much jealous hostility a beautiful, fluent, and popular preacher may arouse in the minds of the hierarchy. It wasn't, he felt, a conversation. It was like flinging oneself into the paddock of a bull that has long been anxious to gore one.

"Inevitably," said the bishop, "this theatricalism, this star-turn business, with its extreme spiritual excitements, its exaggerated soul crises and all the rest of it, leads to such a breakdown as afflicts you. Inevitably! You were at least wise to come to me. I can see you are only in the beginning of your trouble, that already in your mind fresh hallucinations are gathering to overwhelm you, voices, special charges and missions, strange revelations. . . .

I wish I had the power to suspend you right away, to send you into retreat. . . ."

Mr. Parchester made a violent effort to control himself. "But I tell you," he said, "that I saw God!" He added, as if to reassure himself: "More plainly, more certainly, than I see you."

"Of course," said the Bishop, "this is how strange new sects come into existence; this is how false prophets spring out of the bosom of the Church. Loose-minded, excitable men of your stamp——"

Mr. Parchester, to his own astonishment, burst into tears. "But I tell you," he wept, "He is here. I have seen. I know."

"Don't talk such nonsense!" said the Bishop. "There is no one here but you and I."

Mr. Parchester expostulated. "But," he protested, "He is omnipresent."

The Bishop controlled an expression of impatience. "It is characteristic of your condition," he said, "that you are unable to distinguish between a matter of fact and a spiritual truth. . . . Now listen to me. If you value your sanity and public decency and the discipline of the Church, go right home from here and go to bed. Send for Broadhays, who will prescribe a safe sedative. And read something calming and graceful and purifying. For my own part, I should be disposed to recommend the 'Life of Saint Francis of Assisi.'" . . .

12

UNHAPPILY Mr. Parchester did not go home. He went out from the Bishop's residence stunned and amazed, and suddenly upon his desolation came the thought of Mrs. Munbridge. . . .

She would understand. . . .

He was shown up to her own little sitting-room. She had already gone up to her room to dress, but when she heard that he had called, and wanted very greatly to see her, she slipped on a loose, beautiful tea-gown, *négligé* thing, and hurried to him. He tried to tell her everything, but she only kept saying "There! there!" She was sure he wanted a cup of tea, he looked so pale and exhausted. She rang to have the tea equipage brought back; she put the dear saint in an arm-chair by the fire; she put cushions about him, and ministered to him. And when she began partially to comprehend what he had experienced, she suddenly realized that she too had experienced it. That vision had been a brain-wave between their two linked and sympathetic brains. And that thought glowed in her as she brewed his tea with her own hands. He had been weeping! How tenderly he felt all these things! He was more sensitive than a woman. What madness to have expected understanding from the Bishop! But that was just like his unworldliness. He was not fit to take care of himself. A wave of tenderness carried her away. "Here is your tea!" she said, bending over him, and fully conscious of her fragrant warmth and sweetness, and suddenly, she could never afterwards explain why she was so, she was moved to kiss him on his brow. . . .

How indescribable is the comfort of a true-hearted womanly friend! The safety of it! The consolation! . . .

About half-past seven that evening Mr. Parchester returned to his own home, and Brompton admitted him. Brompton was relieved to find his employer looking quite restored and ordinary again.

"Brompton," said Mr. Parchester, "I will not have the usual dinner to-night. Just a single mutton cutlet and one of those quarter-bottles of Perrier Jouet on a tray in my study. I shall have to finish my sermon to-night."

And he had promised Mrs. Munbridge he would preach that sermon specially for her.

13

AND as it was with Mr. Parchester and Brompton and Mrs. Munbridge, and the taxi-driver and the policeman and the little old lady and the automobile mechanics and Mr. Parchester's secretary and the Bishop, so it was with all the rest of the world. If a thing is sufficiently strange and great no one will perceive it. Men will go on in their own ways though one rose from the dead to tell them that the Kingdom of Heaven was at hand, though the Kingdom itself and all its glory became visible, blinding their eyes. They and their ways are one. Men will go on in their ways as rabbits will go on feeding in their hutches within a hundred yards of a battery of artillery. For rabbits are rabbits, and made to eat and breed, and men are human beings and creatures of habit and custom and prejudice; and what has made them, what will judge them, what will destroy them—they may turn their eyes to it at times as the rabbits will glance at the concussion of the guns, but it will never draw them away from eating their lettuce and sniffing after their does. . . .

14

THERE was something of invalid peevishness even in the handwriting of Boon's last story, the Story of the Last Trump.

Of course, I see exactly what Boon is driving at in this fragment.

The distresses of the war had for a time broken down his faith in the Mind of the Race, and so he mocked at the idea that under any sort of threat or warning whatever men's minds can move out of the grooves in which they run. And yet in happier moods that was his own idea, and my belief in it came from him. That he should, in his illness, fall away from that saving confidence which he could give to me, and that he should die before his courage returned, seems just a part of the inexplicable tragedy of life. Because clearly this end of the Story of the Last Trump is forced and false, is unjust to life. I know how feebly we apprehend things, I know how we forget, but because we forget it does not follow that we never remember, because we fail to apprehend perfectly it does not follow that we have no understanding. And so I feel that the true course of the Story of the Last Trump should have been far larger and much more wonderful and subtle than Boon made it. That instant vision of God would not have been dismissed altogether. People might have gone on, as Boon tells us they went on, but they would have been haunted nevertheless by a new sense of deep, tremendous things. . . .

Cynicism is humour in ill-health. It would have been far more difficult to tell the story of how a multitude of commonplace people were changed by a half-dubious perception that God was indeed close at hand to them, a perception that they would sometimes struggle with and deny, sometimes realize overwhelmingly; it would have been a beautiful, pitiful, wonderful story, and it may be if Boon had lived he would have written it. He could have written it. But he was too ill for that much of writing, and the tired pencil turned to the easier course. . . .

I can't believe after all I know of him, and particularly after the intimate talk I have repeated, that he would have remained in this mood. He would, I am certain, have altered the Story of the Last Trump. He must have done so.

And so, too, about this war, this dreadful outbreak of brutish violence which has darkened all our lives, I do not think he would have remained despairful. As his health mended, as the braveries of spring drew near, he would have risen again to the assurance he gave me that the Mind is immortal and invincible.

Of course there is no denying the evil, the black evils of this war; many of us are impoverished and ruined, many of us are wounded, almost all of us have lost friends and suffered indirectly in a hundred ways. And all that is going on yet. The black stream of consequence will flow for centuries. But all this multitudinous individual unhappiness is still compatible with a great progressive movement in the general mind. Being wounded and impoverished, being hurt and seeing things destroyed, is as much living and learning as anything else in the world. The tremendous present disaster of Europe may not be, after all, a disaster for mankind. Horrible possibilities have to be realized, and they can be realized only by experience; complacencies, fatuities have to be destroyed; we have to learn and relearn what Boon once called "the bitter need for honesty." We must see these things from the standpoint of the Race Life, whose days are hundreds of years. . . .

Nevertheless, such belief cannot alter for me the fact that Boon is dead and our little circle is scattered. I feel that no personal comfort nor any further happiness of the mind remains in store for me. My duties as his literary executor still give me access to the dear old house and the garden of our security, and, in spite of a considerable coolness between myself and

THE STORY OF THE LAST TRUMP

Mrs. Boon—who would willingly have all this material destroyed and his reputation rest upon his better-known works—I make my duty my excuse to go there nearly every day and think. I am really in doubt about many matters. I cannot determine, for example, whether it may not be possible to make another volume from the fragments still remaining over after this one. There are great quantities of sketches, several long pieces of Vers Libre, the story of "Jane in Heaven," the draft of a novel. And so I go there and take out the papers and fall into fits of thinking. I turn the untidy pages and think about Boon and of all the stream of nonsense and fancy that was so much more serious to him and to me than the serious business of life. I go there, I know, very much as a cat hangs about its home after its people have departed—that is to say, a little incredulously and with the gleam of a reasonless hope. . . .

There must, I suppose, come a limit to these visitations, and I shall have to go about my own business. I can see in Mrs. Boon's eye that she will presently demand conclusive decisions. In a world that has grown suddenly chilly and lonely I know I must go on with my work under difficult and novel conditions (and now well into the routines of middle age) as if there were no such things as loss and disappointment. I am, I learned long ago, an uncreative, unimportant man. And yet, I suppose, I do something; I count; it is better that I should help than not in the great task of literature, the great task of becoming the thought and the expressed intention of the race, the task of taming violence, organizing the aimless, destroying error, the task of waylaying the Wild Asses of the Devil and sending them back to Hell. It does not matter how individually feeble we writers and disseminators are; we have to hunt the Wild Asses. As the feeblest puppy has to bark at cats and burglars. And we have to do it because we know, in spite of the darkness, the wickedness, the haste and hate, we know in our hearts, though no momentary trumpeting has shown it to us, that judgement is all about us and God stands close at hand.

Yes, we go on.

But I wish that George Boon were still in the world with me, and I wish that he could have written a different ending to the Story of the Last Trump.